D0885003

Your Voice at Its Best

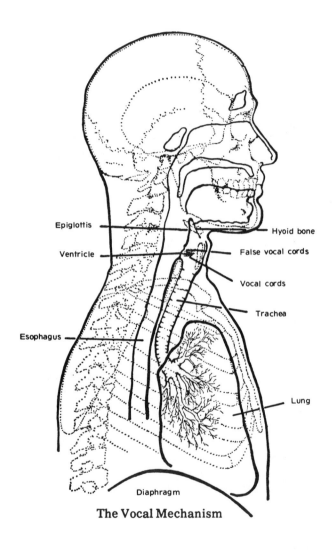

Epiglottis

Ventricle

Esophagus

Hyoid bone

False vocal cords

Vocal cords

Trachea

Lung

Diaphragm

The Vocal Mechanism

YOUR VOICE
At Its Best

David Blair McClosky

ILLUSTRATED BY

William Henry Robinson, III

THE BOSTON MUSIC COMPANY
a Division of Williamson Music, Inc.
116 Boylston St., Boston, Ma 02116

est. 1885

Copyright, (c), 1972, By David Blair McClosky

All rights reserved. No part of this book may be reproduced in any form without permission in writing from the publisher, except by a reviewer who may quote brief passages in a review to be printed in a magazine or newspaper.

First Hard-Cover Edition   1959
Second Hard-Cover Edition   1960
Third Hard-Cover Edition   1962

Hard-Cover Editions

Published by Little Brown & Co.,
Boston, Massachusetts

First Paperback
Edition   1967
Second Paperback
Edition (Revised)   1972
Third Paperback
Edition   1975
Fourth Paperback
Edition (Revised)   1978

Printed in the United States of America

Spanish Edition
Paperback, Argentina   1960
Japanese Edition
Paperback, Tokyo   1974
French Edition   In Progress

Foreword . . .

For some time, I have felt that certain parts of the original text of "Your Voice at Its Best" needed re-editing and amplification. This second paper-back edition has offered just such an opportunity. My general approach to the production and maintenance of a healthy voice —— all the techniques now being used by me and my associates in training singers and speakers or treating patients therapeutically —— are basically the same as before. Research continues, of course (I have added some thoughts particularly to the first five chapters). There is a vast amount yet to be learned about the functions of the larynx.

One criticism which occurs to me concerning this book is that it does not adequately stress the great necessity of the **Frequency of practice** of the exercises indicated so that a singer or public speaker may improve his voice or a therapy patient achieve a healthy larynx. The relaxation and breathing exercises should be practiced often enough each day, in moderate amounts, to make them habitual to everyday life and conversation. It is certainly not enough for a public speaker to try to remember the fundamentals of good phonation only as he is about to step onto the platform for a major speech. Singers, too, are apt to rely more upon the inspiration of the moment than upon a sure technique to carry them through a performance. The techniques of good phonation should be, I reiterate, part of everyday life, a matter of second nature, rather than something called upon hastily at the last minute. The way one makes sounds or breathes properly should become as natural as the way one walks. Techniques for singing and speaking are the same: a good slogan might be, "Sing as you speak — speak as you sing."

Since "Your Voice at Its Best" was first published by Little, Brown & Co. in 1959, I have been privileged to have many students and patients under my guidance. It was a thrilling experience for me to act as vocal advisor to the late President Kennedy on his campaign and to work with him even before that in Hyannisport and Washington. It could be said that this was the challenge of my career — to preserve and enhance the voice of this man, who indeed had lost his voice during the West Virginia primary. Other well-known public persons have kindly shown in their letters and statements included in this new edition that their dedication to the rules, advice and exercises given herein has been the answer to their healthy and improved use of the voice

I should like to reiterate that the techniques described in this volume are in no way contrary to the approach of any conscientious teacher of singing or speech, but represent only a stressing of the actual ground-work necessary to the healthy production of the voice. Many teachers have told me that their students are much more able to apply advanced methods to their study after having read this book.

May I express my gratitude to everyone who made possible the first American and Canadian editions as well as the one in Spanish, published in Argentina, and now this new paper-back edition which should allow these ideas to reach even more people in need of vocal reinforcement or rehabilitation.

It may occur to some readers of this book that if they follow the prescribed exercises, particularly those concerned with articulation, they will achieve a more standard American speech, free of regional dialect. This is not the case. It would be necessary for such readers to go to a speech-coach trained to iron out regional speech-idiosyncrasies to achieve this. I am not particularly concerned with regionalism in speech, unless my student wishes to have a stage career or to learn to sing songs in English with a generally accepted standard pronunciation. Indeed, when President Kennedy was first in office, I took exception to an article in the Sunday **New York Times** which accused the President of regionalism in his speech. I replied. "I see no reason at all why, in his job as President, he should not reflect his regional background in his speech and continue to carry with him the accent with which millions of people in this country and elsewhere associate him. To water this down into a generalized accentless speech would only serve to destroy some of his identity and change his present spontaneity of expression into an over-studied delivery. Let him sound like John F. Kennedy and no one else!" I sent a copy of my letter to the President and his reply was:

"Dear Blair:

It was good to have your letter, and many thanks for taking on **(Author of the New York Times article)** for me. Very well said!

With every good wish,

Sincerely,

John Kennedy"

To Barbara —
without whose collaboration
and patient assistance
this book would not have
been completed

Introduction

THE art of speaking and the closely related art of singing have been practiced for thousands of years and have remained arts. There is no doubt but that man, ever since he first found he could make sounds, has tried to enlarge the possibilities of phonation and enhance the sounds he produced. But in recent years, not much more than a hundred to be exact, a modicum of science has slowly found its way into the art of producing vocal sound, or phonation. Only at this comparatively late date in forensic, dramatic and musical history are we beginning to understand some of the fundamentals on which a sound and lasting ability to speak and sing can be established.

Some temerity is required for anyone to offer even an approach to a better method of phonation. No book can possibly take the place of a good teacher. It would be pretentious indeed to assume that any teacher is qualified as yet to set up a completely new theory of voice reproduction. Nevertheless, in the past few years, with the aid of new techniques and apparatus in related fields, a few things have been learned which can make a meaningful contribution to the body of knowledge which others have accumulated.

To have authority, suggestions for improving the voice should be based on seasoned observation, analysis, and application, not alone by an experienced singer or speaker, but by a teacher who has seen hundreds of his students practice successfully the principles he expounds. The approach offered here is the result of more than fifty years of study, speaking, singing, teaching of students and teachers, and therapeutic work with medical scientists specializing in treatment of the throat and larynx. The studio has been my laboratory and my "guinea pigs" have been singers and speakers, young and old, beginners and veterans.

What are these principles?

First, let me tell you for what purposes this guide has been written and for what groups of persons it has been designed.

My purpose is to provide a simple and clear explanation of the processes involved in correct and therefore healthy and long-lasting vocal-sound production, and how they may be applied by teachers, students, ministers, public speakers and businessmen, as well as by other mature and professional speakers and singers. I include also those who are developing their voices and those who have misused them and need vocal rehabilitation.

Possibly what I have to offer can be most useful to teachers of singing; many of them, I have found, are excellent and thorough musicians, doing a fine job of instruction in expression, interpretation and the coaching of song literature, but actually deficient in their knowledge of the physical facts connected with the singing mechanism. They know what they want to hear in a voice but are not sufficiently schooled in the fundamentals of vocal function. These teachers, I realize, will be slow to adopt any new approach differing from their present method, but I trust will be open-minded enough to weigh my observations with such care as they may merit.

Teachers of speech, I have found, are inclined to differentiate sharply between their own art and the teaching of singing. Nevertheless, correct sound production applies quite as much to the teaching of speech as to the teaching of singing, and there is enough in common between the two to warrant any speech teacher's assimilation of much that I have to submit. Obviously both singing and speaking are produced by the same set of vocal cords, even though they may be motivated by different areas in the brain. It is still true that "well spoken is half sung," and I might add conversely that "singing is speech on pitch."

Even those teachers who do not accept all my principles will find that students who have read this book will have less to **unlearn** and will be more responsive to whatever helpful instruction they are offered than those students who have not been exposed to these preparatory fundamentals.

If you are a student of speech or of singing, I will say to you that this book is no substitute for a good teacher. There is and can be no satisfactory alternative to the personal observation, encouragement and guidance of a knowledgeable instructor. This is a "do-it-yourself" guide only insofar as it will **prepare you to be a better student.** As any honest teacher prefers to work with well-prepared students, so any aspiring student will get more out of his or her instruction when the preliminaries have been understood in advance. These preliminaries need not be tedious and can be fascinating. And, if correctly established, they are one part of the learning program which teachers will prefer to find already accomplished.

It is easy to spoil a good natural voice and there are millions of voices which have been damaged — if very few beyond repair — by faulty training. Any student who reads this will do well to ask himself: "Could my adoption of this approach possibly harm me?" As you read on, your common sense will tell you that proper relaxation of the muscles surrounding the vocal apparatus never harmed anyone and that the other steps described are all in the direction of harmless and constructive progress. You cannot possibly **lose** anything and I can promise you without qualification that if you will read this message thoughtfully and make even a slight effort to put these principles to test and into practice, you will have assisted any teacher of voice or speech to make more rapid and substantial progress with the development of your voice.

In addition to what this book can do for students and teachers, I feel warranted in believing that it can also be of help to throat specialists. For twenty-seven years, I have worked with several otolaryngologists in the therapeutic correction of vocal disorders. Through their interest, guidance, and collaboration I have conducted seminars and lectured before their gatherings and have treated hundreds of cases involving functional and psychological disorders affecting the larynx. One of the things I respect most about the medical profession is that its members never consider that they have arrived at the **ultimate** understanding of the disorders they treat, or feel that there is nothing more for them to learn. Without their interest and help, I would never have had the incentive nor the confidence to work steadily toward surer methods and techniques for improving and rehabilitating the voice.

If you are a singer or a speaker whose voice has deteriorated or is failing, I can say to you with confidence that the unreclaimable voice is rare. With the proper training in the sort of techniques outlined in this book, your voice should not only return to normal but improve and develop. The many faults and bad habits resulting from poor training can usually be remedied easily and few indeed are justified in despairing.

The human voice is an instrument capable of producing the most astonishing range of sounds, colors, emotions and musical tones. It was not intended by nature to make music, or even speech, but has evolved and developed to these capabilities. We have to understand this instrument, its possibilities, limitations and the techniques of using it, quite as clearly as we need to comprehend the workings of a piano, a violin or a clarinet. Because the working of our own instrument is invisible — except as modern science by means of X-ray and slow-motion pictures has visualized it — its functions have until recently been fairly obscure. Therefore, it is not so easy to understand as a man-made instrument which we can look at, touch and examine minutely. The need for understanding is no less, however. The more we know about the human voice and how it functions, the better we shall be able to use it to its fullest as a means of expression.

Every doctor depends on the study of illness, or what he calls **pathology,** to learn more about health. **Therapeutics,** the curative treatment of disease, is facilitated by first knowing exactly what is wrong. So, in singing and speaking, I first came to a clear realization of what I had learned about **correct** vocalization when, in 1946, I had to cure myself on short notice of a vocal weakness which had developed following a long period of illness and convalescence in an Army hospital at Spokane. (I had contracted a severe chest ailment following my transfer from the tropics to a cold climate while in my last year with the Army Air Force during World War II.) I was scheduled to give a song recital at Town Hall in New York City during my first year as a member of the voice faculty at Syracuse University's College of Music. As my rehearsals for this concert went on, I became increasingly aware of the fact that my throat was not in a healthy condition. Apparently I had attempted to resume my singing career too soon following the aforementioned illness, which had confined me for almost a year. My throat specialist, the late Dr. Irl Blaisdell, told me to cancel the recital, as it would be impossible to correct the condition in the fortnight remaining. By this time, however, it was too late to postpone the performance. Then came the supreme test of what I had learned about relaxation, breathing, support, co-ordination and resonance. During those two weeks, I called upon all the knowledge I had of the workings of the voice and put the time which would have ordinarily been spent in rehearsing the recital songs toward light vocal exercises. By the time the recital took place, Dr. Blaisdell declared my larynx to be in normal condition and I was able to proceed with complete confidence. This crisis became a turning point in my life, vocally speaking, leading from there to new developments in vocal therapeutics. What had been only theory had now been tested and proven on my own person in an emergency. From that day to this I have never doubted the efficacy of the curative method I then employed and which I have since developed and practiced for twenty-seven years but which until 1959, and subsequently, I was not ready to publish.

From the many physicians with whom I have worked I have learned caution, patience and humility. Therefore I do not offer **Your Voice at Its Best** as the last work on the subject. Disorders caused by faulty use of the voice, such as chronic laryngitis, vocal nodules and polyps, bowed vocal cords, contact ulcers, use of false cords in phonation, have, time after time, been completely cured. Other pathological conditions, such as hysterical (spastic) dysphonia and aphonia, retarded adolescent or falsetto voice, some forms of paralysis such as might result from a thyroidectomy in which the recurrent laryngeal nerve has been damaged, or laryngo-fissure (in which a vocal cord has been removed) have been cured or definitely helped. However, many more case histories must be added to the substantial number already recorded before I shall feel that I have made a conclusive and lasting contribution to voice therapy.

I am not so modest about what I have learned about the teaching of singing and speaking from my experience and quarter-century of therapeutic practice. **A method which is effective in reclaiming impaired voices must have exceptional merit in maintaining the health of unimpaired ones and allowing them to develop under the best possible conditions.**

Contents

List of Illustrations

Your Voice at Its Best

Chapter 1

Relaxation

PROPER relaxation is the first step to be considered in achieving a truly well-co-ordinated voice. It is the key to all that follows. Until you are able to relax all the muscles in the face, tongue, jaw, chin, throat and neck which interfere with the muscles controlling the vocal cords themselves, your singing and speaking will be muscle-bound.

Every biological function involving the use of muscles depends upon a balance between tension and relaxation. Most of us in using our voices are beset by undue muscular tightness throughout the vocal mechanism — in the throat, jaw, neck, tongue and even in the diaphragm. Unfortunately these tensions are not confined to the areas where they are needed as part of the natural muscular action involved in the activation of the vocal cords. They are apt to predominate in the very areas where there should be the greatest relaxation and looseness. Instead of opening the door and allowing the caged bird, our voice, its freedom, we constrict it with all sorts of fetters. Because to achieve and maintain balanced relaxation is the most vital and difficult physical element in singing and speaking, it is given first emphasis and particular attention.

As you will see later, when reading the Appendix, the muscles of the larynx are generally divided into two groups: those inside the larynx, which directly control phonation (the intrinsic muscles), and those which move the larynx as a whole and keep it suspended in the neck (the extrinsic muscles). It should be our aim to relax the latter set of muscles as well as all the outer muscles above our shoulders and then to maintain this relaxation while we make sounds. By doing this, we are clearing the way to allow the inner muscles of the larynx to function unobstructedly in the production of sound. We need not worry about manipulating the inner muscles which control the vocal cords, for the mere thought of speaking or singing is enough to alert them into functioning, since they operate unconsciously and not by direct manipulation. In a healthy throat, if the outer muscles are relaxed, the inner ones will take care of themselves.

"This is all very well," you may say, "but how am I to know when these outer muscles are really relaxed?" This is easier than it may seem, because it is possible for us to feel most of these muscles with our fingers and to detect tension in them, whereas we may have no tactile contact with the inner muscles. The muscles you can feel with your fingers are the ones which must be relaxed.

It goes almost without saying that before setting about a program of relaxation the student should put himself into the most untrammeled frame of mind possible. Try to feel "asleep on your feet." You are then ready to start a series of very definite exercises to achieve maximum relaxation through the jaw, throat and neck areas. You will find that this adjustment can be made only when a general state of lassitude has been reached.

Long experience has shown that the easiest approach for the student is for him to have his plan of relaxation broken down into six areas, involving as many steps. Every student will not have the same tensions, and in many young people they are difficult to detect. However, if the student does not become aware at the beginning of his study where the danger spot lies, he is all too apt to acquire bad habits and build up tensions which in later years will cause his singing or speaking to be strained. What may seem like a small lack of co-ordination now may, as we grow older, develop into a severe handicap. By following this simple plan, therefore, the student can readily detect and correct his own individual problems.

These exercises are to be used not only **before** one begins to speak or sing, but also **during** vocal exercises, on every vowel, and finally on all pitches. If you can achieve this at the beginning of your study, you will have conquered a major part of your technical trouble at its source. "These exercises are progressive (1) through (6)."

SIX EXERCISES IN RELAXATION

Sit in a comfortable position and try to invite an untroubled state of mind. Do not hurry. Do not press. The essence of these exercises is that they be done slowly, deliberately, without clock-watching.

1. Starting at the hairline and working down to the lower neck, gently massage the muscles of face and throat. As you stroke downwards, allow the face to fall into as limp a condition as possible. Rub the fingers over the eyes, closing them. Let the jaw hang slack.

2. Allow the tongue to fall out over the lower lip as it might if you were unconscious. This means fall; do not push it.

3. This exercise is to relax the **swallowing muscles.** These are attached to the mandible (jawbone) from base to tip and converge upon the hyoid bone at the top of the larynx. (See Figure 6, p. 122). To relax these muscles,

use the fingers of both hands to press gently, on one side and then the other, the soft part of the throat between the chin and the Adam's apple, starting under the hinge of the jaw. Gently massage these muscles until they are soft and pliable, moving the fingers gradually until they are directly under the chin. In this position, swallow, and you will feel downward pressure in the throat. It is vitally important that this area be kept relaxed, soft and pliable during all phases of voice production. This can be checked so easily with the fingers that there is no excuse for tension here.

4. Now take the chin between the thumb and forefinger and move it up and down, at first slowly, then rapidly. If you have been able completely to relax the hinge muscles of the jaw, this exercise will give you no trouble. On first trying it, most persons find, however, that there is resistance in the jaw, particularly when moving it back to a closed position. Involuntarily their jaw muscles are inclined to stiffen. Not until you are able to move your chin freely up and down without the slightest resistance will you have accomplished the aim of this exercise. Maintain all of the relaxation you have established up to this point. Do not permit concentration on one

relaxing exercise to cause you to neglect the others. Above all, **take it easy.**

5. With relaxation of the other areas in mind, take the larynx between the thumb and fingers of one hand and lightly move it from side to side to make sure it floats and does not click. Rigidity here is usually caused by too low or strident a tone of voice.

6. To be sure that the lower neck muscles are relaxed, allow the head to nod up and down lazily while you are maintaining all the other relaxations.

Chapter 2

Breathing

The Singer's—Speaker's Position

AS natural as "breathing" is proverbial, but to the speaker and singer there is a lot more to it than that. Relaxation clears the track for vocalizing but **breath** is the motive power. Without a clear understanding of how to improve on natural respiration, no singer or speaker can be assured of maintaining the needed relaxation, the effortless emission of sound, nor vocal health.

Breathing is one of the few bodily functions which are both unconscious and conscious, involuntary and, within well-defined limits, voluntary. After running or a steep climb, we are conscious of being out of breath. But, generally speaking, we give little thought to breath control. In singing and speaking, however, we have to pay a great deal of attention to it until, through careful thought and with helpful exercises, correct breathing for phonation becomes as automatic as driving a car.

When we are not speaking or singing or thinking about breathing, enough air passes into our lungs without effort to provide the necessary exchange of oxygen for carbon dioxide. As we breathe through our noses, the rhythmic action, controlled by the respiratory center of the brain, goes quietly and uninterruptedly on.

As soon as we open our mouths to sing or speak, however, a different kind of breathing should begin. Our conscious mind is brought into play. We must have enough breath to get through a sentence or a musical phrase without either hesitation or gulping, and perhaps keep this up all evening. Furthermore, we must have enough breath and breath-control to sustain and even amplify our voice while completing a phrase. If we are performing professionally, we must be able to keep on phonating for a long period of time while retaining a fresh, clear and steady voice. This will not be possible if we are constantly gasping for breath or discovering, in the middle of a phrase, that we are "out of gas." Therefore, we must know the components of our breathing apparatus and how to use them. Just as we learn to hold a golf club and perfect our swing to send the ball down the fairway, so must we learn to use all of our breathing muscles in the right co-ordination.

When we breathe for phonation we take in three or four times as much air as for passive breathing. And it no longer flows in and out rhythmically, since we exhale much more slowly than we inhale. One of the chief aims in learning to breathe consciously is to replenish our breath quickly and effortlessly without disturbing the flow of our spoken or musical meaning and then to propel our breath gradually and under complete but relaxed control, and to finish each phrase in the most telling manner. Breath pressure will, of course vary greatly according to the volume and quality of sound produced.

Our breathing apparatus consists of the lungs, with their surrounding rib cage, layered inside and out with muscles; the diaphragm and abdominal muscles; and the passages which carry air to mouth and nose, consisting of the bronchi, the trachea or windpipe, the larynx and the pharynx. (See the Frontispiece.) Entirely aside from its helpful and necessary effect on producing sound, the full development of breathing power makes for general health and well-being. Deep breathing has long been recognized as one of the most salutary physical habits. The extra oxygen taken in with a deep breath purifies the blood and gives us extra energy. Many people go through life without ever taking a really deep breath except when violent exercise forces them to do so. Physicians tell us that asthmatic conditions can often be alleviated by deep-breathing exercises. And every athlete knows that his capacity to perform at his best depends in large part on his ability to supply himself with the needed extra oxygen.

The ribs are flexible. They consist of twelve pairs (See Figure 1, p. 13) joined to the backbone and connected to the breastbone (sternum) by cartilages, except for the two floating ribs at the bottom, which are joined to the abdominal wall by bands of connective tissue. The muscles inside the ribs are called **intercostals;** those outside go by the same name or are known as **costal levators.** These names indicate the functions of these muscles, since **costa** is Latin for rib. The inside muscles go between the ribs, connecting them and contracting when we exhale. The outside rib muscles raise the ribs when we take a breath and expand our chest. Shallow breathing is confined to the chest and most persons in ordinary breathing depend upon the rib muscles and make little use of the more powerful abdominal muscles. But it is the abdominal muscles which speakers and singers need to develop. (See Figure 2, p. 15.)

Of the lower muscles, the **diaphragm** is the most important single factor in controlling breathing. This partition, which separates our chest or thorax from our abdomen, consists almost entirely of muscles which come together to a tendon at the center. Though elastic, the diaphragm is very powerful. When at rest, it has the

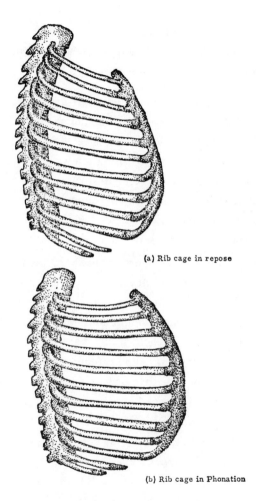

(a) Rib cage in repose

(b) Rib cage in Phonation

FIG. 1. Rib Cage in Repose and in Position
for Phonation

shape of an inverted bowl, but when we take a deep breath, it flattens. (See Figure 3, p. 16.)

Although the diaphragm action is up and down, rising and falling as we breathe, we do not see its action. What we see is its effect on the walls of the abdomen, which extend and retract in co-ordination with the diaphragm. As we breathe in, our waist gets larger; as we exhale, our abdomen resumes its former shape. Several abdominal muscles, horizontal, vertical and oblique, assist the diaphragm in pushing out the breath.

Few professional singers or speakers have tiny waists, but they do have well-developed diaphragms and strong abdominal walls. Curiously, clavicular or upper-chest breathing is actually taught in some schools. Students are told to draw in their stomachs and throw out their chests while standing with stiffened shoulders like West Point cadets. Such breathing is favored by those to whom a small waist is more important than a good voice or good health. And such vanity is not confined to feminine students but finds favor among some men, whose ideal of manly beauty requires a wasp waist, broad shoulders and slim hips. It can be said with finality that the student who is content to confine his breathing to his upper chest will not and cannot enjoy the full potentialities of his voice.

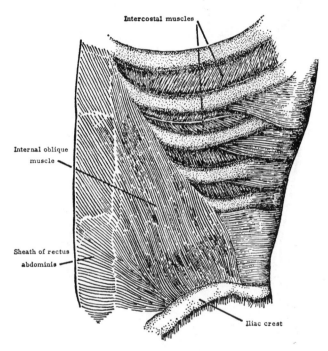

Intercostal muscles

Internal oblique
muscle

Sheath of rectus
abdominis

Iliac crest

FIG. 2. Abdominal and Rib-Action Muscles

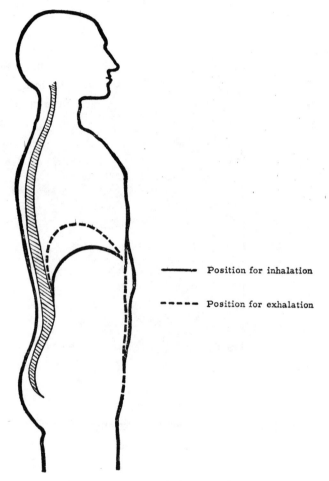

_____ Position for inhalation

- - - - - Position for exhalation

FIG. 3.   Action of the Diaphragm

Proper posture is the first answer to proper functioning of the voice and breath control. As a Boston voice-teacher named Charles Adams White said to me on his eightieth birthday in 1925, "Remember, McClosky, the rule my old teacher Francesco Lamperti gave me years ago! 'You do not sing yourself — your body sings you!' When I came to realize the fullest meaning of this some years later, I began to sing at my best. The posture I am about to discuss will **allow** your body to function at its best for your singing. It may seem unnatural to you at first, but as you use it day after day you will find that with it basically maintained, you can run, jump, bend, act on stage, or engage in sports and have no feeling of stiffness or discomfort.

To arrive at the proper posture, **stand up straight, one foot slightly in advance** of and **apart from the other. Lightly dig in your toes** as if to grasp the floor with them. Tuck your hips under without allowing the upper part of your body to **change its position.** This will tend to keep your **knees from locking** (they should be just **slightly bent).** Next, squeeze the buttocks together and stretch the muscles of the **lower back** from the tip of the spine to the point of their attachment to the **lower ribs.** This action should make you feel an expansion of the lower ribs at the back and a drawing in of the pelvic muscles. **Keep**

this posture. Now you should feel the weight of your body **evenly distributed** between the toes and the heels.

Then, allow the breath to come in through the **nose** with the **mouth slightly open.** (Remember, concentrate on the passage of air through the nose; enough air will find its way through the mouth.) If your posture has been maintained, you should feel the **abdominal wall** expand, front and sides with **no action of the ribs,** which, as you recall, you have been maintaining in an expanded position. Remember to concentrate on your **complete** posture. In the final analysis, no conscious action should cause the breath to enter or leave the body. This becomes an automatic action, the amount of breath being used entirely determined by the length of the spoken or sung phrase and its dynamics. Your conscious effort must for a long time be directed toward your posture or position of your body. Your breath will enter your body easily and leave it in the same way. This will become a completely subconscious action at the beginning of and during phonation.

EXERCISE FOR STRENGTHENING
THE INTERCOSTAL MUSCLES

Lean over, grasping your bent knees. Take a large deep breath abdominally and keep it. Then, rise on your toes and draw in your abdominal muscles strongly, arching your back with your head down. Now, without releasing your breath, spring up from your knees and toes, feeling a strong upward pressure in your back rib muscles. Repeat this several times without breathing. This will strengthen the muscles used for resisting any collapse of the chest.

This chapter should make it clear that we must beware of the teaching method expressed in the too-often-heard advice: "Oh, just breathe naturally!" What is meant by **naturally?** Some students "naturally" breathe more deeply than others. A few singers and speakers eventually achieve abdominal breathing unconsciously, due to the demands made upon their voices. They learn the hard way that they cannot get enough breath or retain it sufficiently when breathing high in the chest. From long experience I have learned that abdominal breathing does **not** come naturally to most students and that, more than any other fault, superficial breathing stands in the way of their progress.

Correct breathing has a scientific basis, and when it becomes second nature, as it does with sufficient practice, we learn to co-ordinate it with the other elements of phonation and then attain the freedom we need in order to turn our attention to voice support, expression and interpretation.

Chapter 3

Co-ordination of Relaxation, Breathing, and Support

ASSUMING that by this time you have learned how to relax and breathe properly, the next step is to apply what you have learned to the producing of vocal sound. At the end of this chapter a simple exercise in phonation is given.

These early chapters are intended to make the work of your teacher easier by giving you advance insight into what is expected of you and what you in turn can expect of your vocal and breathing mechanisms. It goes without saying that you will gain by having a competent teacher at hand to observe and supervise the progress you have made due to the instructions already given, and, more particularly, from the precepts which follow. Any process involving physical co-ordination calls for the services of a skilled second party to bring the technique alive, by observation of what you are doing, by correction of your mistakes, and best of all, by correct example.

In this chapter, we are considering the complete action of phonation, that is, harmoniously functioning relaxation and breathing coupled with an added element which we call **support**. After you have mastered relaxation in the six areas mentioned and have learned to combine posture, diaphragm action and rib-cage resistance in breathing, your next step is to use what you have learned to improve your speaking and singing voice. It is not enough merely to produce a pleasant sound. This sound must be controlled, supported and sustained, and, in doing this correctly you will call upon the action of a combination of the rib muscles of the back, the pelvic muscles, the gluteal muscles (buttocks) and leg muscles running all the way down to the toes gripping the floor.

As you can see, the foregoing instructions are all directed toward control for the purpose of keeping the breath in steady and constant supply during speaking and singing. For some time, this will be a conscious act of co-ordinating, but with faithful practice it will gradually become second nature. Obviously such mastery cannot be developed overnight. The speaker, unless he is holding daily revival meetings, conducting auctions, giving pep talks, has a big part in a play, or otherwise makes sustained, daily use of his voice, will require a shorter period of training. The singer, however, is in for a protracted regimen of practice to strengthen and control all the muscles used in a finished performance.

Do not attempt short cuts. Do not expect to accomplish in a week what will require a year or more of close application. To produce a completely sound singing technique, several years of well-co-ordinated practice and muscular development will be needed. Your body will need to have reached its full maturity as well. During this period of development, the attention and advice of an experienced teacher are indispensable.

Exercises

Take the proper posture as described on page 17; making sure that all areas of relaxation have been checked. Draw in a breath predominantly through the nose with the mouth open. Allow the breath to go out the same as it was drawn in and with no change of body or mouth position. Repeat several times. You will realize, of course, that the rib-muscles at the back should still be stretched, never relaxing their firmness, and therefore, leaving the action of breathing to the diaphragm, abdominal wall and lower supporting muscles.

Now, with a vowel-sound in your mind (think "ah" for example) take in another breath. Emit it as a singing-sound on the "ah," with no change of position of the body or mouth and being sure to feel the predominance of the air passing out through the nose. As you sustain the sound, you will feel all the elements of your breath-support gradually being brought into play — the back-rib-muscle action, maintaining the rib-cage in its original posture position — the squeezing of the buttocks-muscles, the feeling of increased muscle-tension going down the legs, the toes gripping more firmly into the floor, and, of course, the diaphragm returning to its raised position as before a breath is taken. You will be feeling an accentuation of the original posture itself, causing the body to "sing you." Further exercises for phonation will be found in Chapter 5.

Chapter 4

Resonance and Color

As speech and singing-teachers we are, obviously, trying to teach our students how to speak and sing. But, on what basis?

Shall we first discuss the artistic results we wish to achieve? Shall we begin by speaking of tone-color, expressive dynamics and style? **Or,** shall we first approach phonation as an "athletic event," a physical training of our body, to make it into as perfect an instrument as we can, for the purpose of expressing ourselves artistically?

Too many teachers, I feel, put the cart before the horse. They do not give students an adequate knowledge of their instrument and **how it works** and how to work **it** before asking them to use it as a means of expression. No skater competing in the Olympics would be asked to go out on the ice and perform complicated figures without a long period of training to make his body ready to respond to the task.

Through their vibration, our vocal cords produce tones but our voice quality is greatly enhanced and given character, color and beauty by the overtones which are produced as our vocal sounds vibrate throughout the cavities in our head and above and below the larynx, as well as by the added vibration of the bony structures surrounding these cavities. Without the added vibration of these auxiliary parts, our vocal sounds would be thin and uninteresting indeed. We need resonance to give richness, amplification and extension to the original sound. We may liken the head cavities and bony parts which make for resonance to the sounding board of a piano or the box of a stringed instrument like a violin or cello. Without their resonators, you would actually not recognize the sounds made by these instruments.

When we speak of the color of a vocal sound, we are actually considering two things: (1) the **natural timbre** or **quality** of the voice, resulting from the physical structure of the larynx and all the resonators, and (2) the kinds of sound resulting from some manipulation on our part of these resonators. To illustrate the difference, we might speak of the dark, rich color of a voice like that of Leonard Warren; or we might refer to a singer's performance as demonstrating a remarkable **change of color** consciously effected by him to suit the mood of two songs of totally different character. A performer like Ruth Draper used change of voice color as her very stock in trade to bring alive to us all the dozens of widely divergent characters she portrayed. This latter technique is the most difficult for a singer to learn to use properly. It has equal importance for an actor or for anyone who wishes to convey a variety of moods and meanings or sway an audience emotionally with his voice. To consider first the natural resonance we desire to bring into our voices: our chief difficulty as beginning students of voice is that, to paraphrase Robert Burns, no power has given us the giftie to hear ourselves as others hear us. At no time are we able to hear the compiete quality of our voice as we are uttering it. We hear not one but two voices: the sound emerging from our mouth and nose and also the sound inside our head of the resonance resulting from the vibration of its chambers and bones. This combination produces a far different effect from the sound which our listeners hear. We hear both inside and outside, so to speak, but never the sound which is transmitted to the far side of the auditorium. Many of us have had our voices recorded for the first time and scarcely recognized that they actually belonged to us, on hearing the play-back. Also, even the highest fidelity in recording does not sound **exactly** like the sound we hear in a room or hall where a performance is going on. It is vital, therefore, that we as speakers or singers in the initial stages of our development have someone of taste, understanding and technical knowledge of the voice to tell us whether or not we are making the most of our phonating apparatus. As we advance, we become used to the sound which our experienced and competent teacher has told us is the best we can make, and we learn to go largely by the feeling we experience in our throat and resonators and not by listening to ourselves. Before they learn to do this, students frequently complain that their newly released voices sound too "nasal" to themselves. This is natural in the beginner who is first experiencing relaxed and easy voice production. His complete voice is emerging for the first time, through an open nasal passage as well as through his mouth. The sound may seem excessively "brassy" to him, since he has usually been so accustomed to making and listening to a sound which probably seemed quite beautiful to him, although it would not have carried across the room. For the first time, he begins to experience the use of nasal and nasopharyngeal resonance in the right way and can hardly believe that to his listeners his voice is merely taking on the clarity, richness and carrying power which it lacked before. He must allow himself to become acquainted with this strange new sound and above all to the freedom he is experiencing in his throat. He will almost have to take it on faith from his teacher that he is now beginning to make the right vocal sounds, and then his own ears will become attuned to them and he will realize that his voice has new-found carrying qualities.

The worst mistake we can make as **beginners** is to try consciously to manipulate our sound-making apparatus to imitate vocal qualities and characteristics we admire in others. Our voice is our own. Like fingerprints, there are no two exactly alike and such individuality is the chief charm of a voice. We have all known beginning students of voice, I am sure (and perhaps have been guilty of this ourselves) who listened to great singers or actors either in person or by means of recordings and tried to imitate their style and particularly their voice quality. The dangers in this should be obvious; the student cannot bypass a real understanding of his own limitations and potentialities by trying to appropriate the tone quality of someone with a different anatomy. He must realize that the most important task ahead of him is to express his own voice personality by allowing his voice to emerge untrammeled by artificial tensions or manipulation of his articulators **before** he has achieved clear understanding of the more fundamental aspects of voice production. If he will concentrate on **these** instead he will be surprised and delighted to find that added resonance he did not possess at the beginning is gradually beginning to enhance his voice and give it better quality and greater size. Resonance will come of its own accord when the relaxation, right breathing and support already described allow the voice to emerge easily and in a free-flowing manner. One great obstruction to the maintenance of an even resonance or focus throughout the vocal line is mouthing. By this I mean an overuse of jaw-action in singing. This serves only to distort vowel sounds and make it difficult for the singer to articulate consonants in time and with clarity.

We come now to the matter of **change of color** in the voice. The student should take the preceding advice in this chapter thoroughly to heart before considering the matter. By it we mean that the shape of our resonating cavities is actually being altered by us to produce different overtones and thereby different tonal effects. Resonating areas can change or be changed to produce many variations of sound and thereby to portray a great variety of specific meanings and moods in a song or reading. When an experienced actor gives a reading which involves more than one role, he is constantly changing the shape of his resonators to produce different effects, clearly indicating to his audience the different characters he is impersonating. When an experienced singer performs Schubert's "The Erlking," he must frequently change his voice quality to indicate the four roles of the Erlking, the father, the son and the narrator. By **thinking** these changes, a well co-ordinated singer automatically takes on the vocal personalities of different characters, but he is far enough **advanced in his technique** to realize consciously that he is helping these changes in color by easy manipulation of the throat and soft palate in particular, as well as of the other articulators and the mouth as a whole. He has already learned that he must retain relaxation in the six areas previously mentioned and any manipulation of muscles is effected with the least possible effort. Thus we see that the time comes when conscious manipulation of the resonators is not only desirable but a necessary part of the art and technique of a singer or speaker. The great danger in this lies in any student's using it **before** he understands the difference between his **own natural voice quality** and **change of vocal color** used for a special effect at a special time. If such manipulation is attempted before the student has gradually and fully developed the natural use of his resonators as part of his general vocal development, he will only defeat his own ends. Such refinements cannot be forced, they must come about as the logical and inevitable result of careful study under the watchful guidance of a fine teacher.

Chapter 5

Exercises for Phonation

AT first glance, the six exercises given in this chapter would seem to follow logically Chapter 3 on the co-ordination of relaxation, breathing and support. However, before a student is asked to make sounds as phonating exercises, it is better that he understand the complete mechanism of his sound-producing system, including breathing and its support.

After you get beyond the initial exercises given here and begin to say or sing syllables and then words, you should be certain that with each sound you make, you are focusing your eyes upon a distant object. You should also use a mirror to sing or speak to, as an aid in projecting your voice and also to detect any strange habits involving facial grimaces or neck tensions. You must begin to consider your vocal efforts as a form of expression, exposition or declaration. In other words, you do not make a study of phonation simply to speak or sing to yourself. You make sounds to **project your voice and**

your ideas, be they dramatic, political or musical, to other people.

Our first step toward correct phonation will consist of the emission of a very breathy, audible sigh, as mentioned in Chapter 3. Almost all of us have a tendency to bring into play, consciously or unconsciously, some of the extrinsic throat muscles which act to make the vocal cords approximate too closely (interfere with each other) when they are in vibration. The sigh we suggest will cause somewhat more breath than usual to pass between the cords while a light sound is being made, and therefore assure the student that the cords are vibrating slightly apart as they should to maintain vocal health and good phonation.

The student must not **force** air between the cords in this case, but **allow it to escape** in the most relaxed and lazy manner imaginable. After you have achieved true coordination of your vocal mechanism, you will no longer need to use this artificial method of assuring that the cords do not come together too closely. Your inner laryngeal muscles will have been strengthened and will have acquired the proper tonus to keep the cords vibrating at the optimum distance apart at all times.

THE EXERCISES

1. Take a breath and expel about half of it before making a sound. Now interrupt the expulsion of air with a

very lazy and light sighing sound on **hah,** beginning in the upper middle part of your voice and inflecting downward, the same as in Chapter 3. Repeat this several times, checking carefully all six areas of relaxation, as well as your breathing and support.

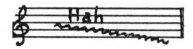

EX. 1

2. Repeat this exercise but with this difference: when you begin to sigh, allow your lips to open and close several times. The result will be a light hum. Do not think of this as an attempt to form the letter **m,** however. Simply feel that you are interrupting the sigh, in which your mouth is slightly open, by drawing the lips together several times until the breath has been expelled. Make as loosely formed a consonant sound as possible; do not bring your lips together firmly to form a tense **m.** The **m** used in this way helps the student immeasurably to begin to think in terms of syllables, made up of both vowel and consonant sounds. The **m** is a voiced consonant,* which means that while it is being pronounced, the vocal cords are vibrating. It is formed at the very front of the mouth

*See Chapter 6, page 49.

without involving any other articulators such as the tongue or hard palate. It in no way has a tendency to disturb the desired relaxation when uttered as suggested:

ah (Father)

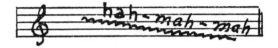

EX. 2

3. Repeat Exercise 2, but change the vowel sounds this time by making a pattern of the sounds "mah-may-mee-mo-moo." Make very effort to maintain each vowel sound on its initial form as you would **say** it, without allowing it to become a diphthong:

$\bar{A}$-(*Gate*)-$\bar{E}$-(*Meet*)-$\bar{O}$-(*Go*)-$\overline{OO}$-(*Food*)

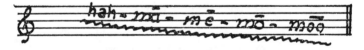

EX. 3

4. This time, use the same downward inflection, saying the words "How-are-you." Do not be disturbed by the fact that your voice has a very "sing-song" quality. That

Mah   May   Mee   Mō   Moo

EX. 4

is exactly what you want at this stage. You are beginning to feel what it is to make relaxed vocal sounds, and have progressed to saying words in this way. Your only concern should be with the **feeling in your throat** as you make these sounds. If they are being produced completely without strain, you will have no feeling there at all.

5. Repeat Exercise 3, this time using a definite pitch-level in the lower-middle part of your voice. Start on about **d** for high voices and **b** for low voices, and **sing** the vowel sounds instead of saying them. Continue this exercise by raising the pitch-level by whole or half steps, sustaining all the sounds on each pitch in turn, without progressing out of the middle part of the voice.

Suggested vowel-combinations

for use in these exercises

EX. 4

6. When you have reached this point and have a fair assurance that you are maintaining the proper relaxation throughout the middle part of the voice on all vowel sounds, combined with proper breath action, you are ready to begin singing slow five-tone scales or short arpeggios on the same sounds and then longer scales and more complicated exercises. So long as you **make sure not to go beyond the point where you can maintain your relaxation,** you will be acquiring the proper technique for using your voice and will not be trying to cover ground too quickly. (See examples).

We have merely touched on the basic exercises to be used while you are still very much concentrating upon the areas of relaxation and the proper techniques of breathing which were discussed earlier. To proceed from this point with more complicated exercises the student

Ah (Father) Ā (Gate) Ē (Meet) Ō (Go) OO (Food)

Vocalises

Make sure not to go beyond the point

where you can maintain your relaxation.

Vocalises

MEN'S Voices

Make sure not to go beyond the point

where you can maintain your relaxation.

needs the guidance of an experienced teacher. **Chapter 6** following will, however, amplify the foregoing with helpful exercises in articulation.

Now an exercise to bridge the gap between singing and speaking:

Start as shown below on the words "How are you today?", **singing** first then repeating five times, slowly changing to **speaking** at the same general pitch-level:

Women's voices   Men's voices

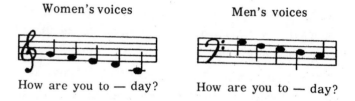

How are you to — day?   How are you to — day?

Try this same singing-speaking approach to all the exercises starting on **page 52**.

This is the correct way to reach optimum pitch.

Chapter 6

Articulation

SINCE vowel sounds are the best vehicles for relaxed phonation, this book has thus far been concerned only with them. If you have read closely, you must by this time have a pretty fair idea of how to project vowel sounds effectively and with due regard for the health of your phonating mechanism.

We have only to say "Good morning!" to the milkman, however, to realize that no one can communicate adequately by means of vowel sounds alone. We utter scarcely any sounds, except perhaps a delighted exclamation, or an interjection to express pain or some other emotion which spills out of us (and some of these we do not use in language at all) without employing consonants as well as vowels. A famous teacher writing late in the last century, Edmund J. Myer, said, "Consonants are the **bones** of speech." He could not have said it more aptly, for without consonants there **is** no speech. Those who think they can slur over their consonants in singing or speaking are failing to utilize one of the most important assists in vocal communication and expression.

How often we are prompted to ask a friend, "What did you say?" when he seems to be speaking in a **loud** enough voice. And how many times have we attended recitals, lectures or plays during which we had to strain our ears to understand the performer. Neglect of consonant articulation is not the only fault which may handicap a speaker or singer and annoy his audience, but it is by all odds the most prevalent omission. If the "bones" of phonation are neglected, the listener can spend the whole evening guessing how to fill in the gaps between the vowel sounds.

With the exception of the resonance chambers, up to now we have been confining our remarks about voice production to the larynx and areas below it. But the human voice is the only musical "instrument" which can combine the meaning of speech with the meaning of music by means of words, and words without consonants are few and fiat. So the time has come to "raise our sights" and discuss how the vowel sounds which we have learned can be combined with all of the needed consonant sounds by means of tongue, hard and soft palate, lips and teeth — the **articulators.**

We can tell by the tone of its voice whether an animal is

frightened or happy, or perhaps is sounding a warning. It can register its emotion, but communication stops there; it cannot tell us the source of its joy, fear or pain, or what it wants us to do about it. It takes both tone **and words** to convey meaning. Man's chief distinction is that he is the **talking animal,** but this achievement means little if he relies on vowels alone. It takes **words,** added to change of color, to form a truly differentiated interpretation of meanings and moods, and this point seems to have escaped many singers and speakers who are capable of showing change of emotion in **sound,** but are unable to communicate adequately because of careless enunciation.

Having practiced the complete relaxation I have urged thus far, the reader may well feel that if and when he enunciates clearly, he may endanger the nice framework for phonation which he has achieved, and may trip over all sorts of tensions which may develop to interfere with the best voice production. That is the reason for this chapter on articulation — the use of the organs and musculature above the larynx in interrupting the flow of vibrating breath to form the various sounds we recognize as consonants. (Strictly speaking we should acknowledge that vowels, too, are articulated, but only as the articulating organs act naturally to change the size and shape of the resonating cavities to differentiate the vowel sounds.)

The tongue, lips and palates assume different adjustments in relation to each other so that they act as valves whose opening and shutting form consonants. These adjustments can be classified in many and complicated ways, but we can simplify them by observing that they are characterized particularly in three ways:

1. Position

2. Whether accompanied or not by vibration of the vocal cords

3. Duration

POSITION

In discussing the positions of the articulators it will help to simplify by dividing the consonants into those which are produced by the action of the lips and are therefore called **labials,** and those produced by the action of the tongue, called **linguals.**

The **labials** in turn may be divided into two groups:

1. Those in which the **lips alone** are used, as in the following examples:

w	win
wh	which
m	meet
p	pork
b	bee

2. Those in which the **lips** are used in conjunction with the **teeth:**

f	father
v	very

The **linguals** may be divided into four groups:

1. Those formed by **tongue** and **teeth:**

th   thick   that

2. Those formed by the **tip of the tongue** and the **hard palate:**

t	tip
d	do
n	no
l	lip
r	row

3. Those formed by the **body of the tongue** and the **hard palate:**

s	sow
z	zebra
sh	show
3 *	azure

4. Those formed by the **body of the tongue** and the **soft palate:**

c	cat
k	king
g	get
ng	sing
y	yes

H is rather special as it is produced simply by breath passing between the vocal cords.

WHETHER ACCOMPANIED BY VIBRATION OF THE VOCAL CORDS

You have undoubtedly noticed that although some of the above sounds are produced by the same articulators,

* 3 is the international phonetic alphabet symbol used to indicate the sound zh as in **pleasure, azure, Asia.**

they nevertheless do not sound alike — instance; **thick** and **that.** This brings us to the second factor involved in the characterization of consonants: whether they are **voiced** (sonants) or **unvoiced** (surds). A voiced consonant is one whose pronunciation is accompanied by vibration of the vocal cords:

b	bead	**w**	west
d	deed	**m**	me
g	good	**n**	not
v	virtue	**l**	lot
th	this	**r**	red
z	zoo	**y**	year
3	azure	**ng**	sing

An **unvoiced** consonant is one which is emitted without any accompanying vibration of the vocal cords:

c	cow	**th**	thought
p	pea	**s**	sea
t	tea	**sh**	shy
k	key	**wh**	which
f	fall	**h**	hot

DURATION

The third factor in determining the quality of a consonant is the length of time involved in its emission. Consonants either stop abruptly, in which case they are called **stops,** or they continue and are therefore called **continuants.**

Stops:

p	ape	**d**	date
b	bottle	**k**	kite
t	at	**g**	gate

Continuants:

w	we	**r**	rose
wh	where	**s**	seal
m	music	**sh**	shower
f	fate	**z**	zealous
v	leave	**3**	azure
th	those thistle	**y**	you
n	nice	**ng**	song
l	leap	**h**	horse

Needless to say, this is a very simplified classification of consonants, but it should suffice for the reader to understand what is involved in their **formation**. You will notice that we are concerned not with spelling but with sound, since **cat** and **kite** are initially the same phonetically, just as **leisure** and **azure** and **garage** all contain the same sound — 3.

For the pronunciation of consonants as exercises, begin by establishing the same conditions of relaxation and co-ordination which I have set forth up to this time. After you have satisfied yourself that you are ready for correct phonation, practice at first only the few words which I have used as examples in the foregoing. You will see that, no matter how much you move your lips (as for example in **which** or **west**) it will be unnecessary to disturb the relaxation of the extrinsic muscles of the throat. Now try saying or singing, **mah-nah-ng-ah** slowly. These sounds start at the front of the mouth using only the lips and proceed from there to the use of the tongue, first employing its tip in conjunction with the hard palate, then its body in connection with the soft palate. You will notice that no matter how fast you say or sing these sounds, it is possible — as it is imperative — to maintain freedom throughout the throat.

Following the order given in the simple outline of consonant characteristics, I have set forth below a series of sentences, designed to make specific use of one set of articulators. These may well remind you of the days of your childhood when you tried to say as fast as you could without stuttering: "He thrusts his fists against the posts and still insists he sees the ghosts," or "Peter Piper picked a peck of pickled peppers." They are not designed as tongue twisters, however, nor are they in any sense corrective exercises for those with speech difficulties. Since this book is not concerned solely with the vast and complex subject of speech, I can deal with it but lightly within the confines of a single chapter. For more specialized exercises or further reading about speech, speech disorders, and correction, I refer you to the several excellent works dealing with these subjects listed in the bibliography.

To begin with the articulation of the **lips,** try saying the following sentence clearly and distinctly and **slowly** at first, being sure to maintain throat relaxation while speaking the words without overexaggerating the movements of the mouth:

1.w **A coward weeps and wails with woe when his wiles are thwarted.**

Now try this one, observing the difference in effect through lack of vocal cord vibration, although the same articulators are working:

2. wh **Which whelp whined when he heard the whale wheeze?**

Notice that both times the consonant sound was a **continuant.**

Still employing the **lips** specifically, say the following sentence, observing that the consonant sound is both **voiced** and a **continuant:**

3. m **Men and women may swim in the warm summertime before September storms come upon them.**

The following two sentences again contain words requiring **lip** action, but both consonants are **stops.** The **b,** however, is voiced, while the **p** is not:

4. b. **The big, bold baboon grabbed the bare branches with his bony, brown hands.**

5. p **The pelican's pouch is primarily appropriate for keeping him supplied with supper.**

The following sentences still involve the use of the **lips** but in conjunction with the **teeth.** Notice the difference in effect between the unvoiced **f** sounds and the voiced **v**'s:

1. f **Five elephants huffed and puffed as they filed through the Friday traffic followed by a laughing waif.**

2. v **Vivacious voices strove to give more volume to the various verses.**

The next sentences call attention to the linguals of the first group: those formed by the interaction of **tongue** and teeth. the first sentence uses **unvoiced** sounds, the next one, **voiced** sounds:

1. th **A thousand thoughts about birth and death came thronging to the mind of the thin, unhealthy youth.**

2. th **They scythed the withering grass beside the smooth paths.**

Our next examples point up the use of the **tip of the tongue** and the **hard palate.** As you read these phrases aloud, try to think carefully about the use of the articulators mentioned and be sure to maintain as much relaxation as possible through the entire throat area so that the articulators may remain flexible and you will feel in no way "tongue-tied" when you have finished. Refer to the preceding outline if you are uncertain as to the special character of the consonant being illustrated; that is, whether it is a sonant or a surd, a stop or a continuant:

1. t **Try to take the time to teach Patty a pleasant tune.**

2. ch **Cheerful Cheshire cats chew chunks of chopped chicken and choke down chestnuts and cheese.**

You will feel when speaking this sentence that your tongue is still using its **tip** for pronunciation of the **ch,** but it also uses its **body** in relation to the hard palate. This, then, is a combination of the sounds of **t** and **sh.**

3. d **Day after day, the good old educators tried to din adequate knowledge into dreamy dunces.**

4. n **An honest scientist needs no hindrance in his sound investigation into the wonders of the universe.**

5. l **Violins and lutes played lovely tunes as the pale silver moonlight filtered through the olive trees.**

6. r **Ripe, round, bright, red berries drenched with rich cream provide thorough pleasure to those who truly relish fruit.**

Try saying this last sentence aloud, first using a trilled **r,** which involves repeated use of the tongue in contact with the hard palate. Then notice the difference when you read it using the standard American **r,** which actually involves the raising of the tongue to the roof of the mouth. Avoid using the lips to pronounce **r;** this is not necessary. Depending on whether you are a singer or a public speaker, or a radio announcer or an actor, or if you wish simply to give particular emphasis to a word here or there, you may find yourself using the trilled **r.** Singers especially find that it can help enormously to clarify a word if used initially, and that it provides a quick springboard to a following vowel when used in the body of a word. You will notice that French singers use it when **singing** their own songs, although they **speak** with an **r** which is pronounced far back in the throat, almost gargled, in fact. Americans should learn to use the trilled **r,** but be careful to use it judiciously and not in such a way as to sound exaggerated or affected.

The next five sentences illustrate the interaction of the **body of the tongue** and the **hard palate.**

1. s **Susan sighed softly as she passed the nice Swiss physicist in the passageway.**

2. z **At the zoo the lazy visitors observed zebras, gazelles, lizards, and prize lions.**

3. sh **She shed her mesh shoes and shamelessly shook her freshly washed shawl from her shoulders.**

4. zh or ʒ **We usually derive composure and pleasure from leisure.**

5. dzh or dʒ **The jealous major became enraged at the adjutant's jolly jokes about his huge budget.**

Coming to the use of the **body of the tongue** in conjunction with the **soft palate,** try the following:

1. c and k. **The kindly king and his quiet queen liked pickled pig's-knuckles with their cooked cabbage and crusty kidney pie.**

2. g **The gay ghost ogled the gaping guests, then wagged**

its gray finger at them as it gathered the garnets together.

3. ng **Bring me a spring song to sing for the waiting throng.**

Now notice the difference in pronunciation of the ng sound in the next sentence, where it is necessary to follow it with an additional sound of g:

4. ng **The distinguished Englishman learned the Anglo-Saxon language and wrote singular jingles in it.**

In the sentence below, we hear the ng sound again, but this time with a following k:

5. ngk **The monkey blinked and wrinkled his pink nose as he tinkled the clinking trinkets on his ankles.**

6. y **Last year the yew in the canyon beyond your yard turned yellow.**

7. h (Be careful not to gargle it.) **Harry the hunter hasn't hiked home through the hills since he heard that a huge horse's hoofprint was beheld in Hiram's Hollow.**

As you can see, an enormous number of possible consonant combinations exists at the beginning, middle, or end of words. It would require an entire volume to list them with examples. Make your own combinations. Start composing sentences using specific combinations, and afterward, reading them for your own study, try speaking them aloud as if you were addressing an audience. Do not use any greater dynamics when speaking or singing these exercises than necessary to cause the sound to vibrate well. Also, try to minimize as much as possible closure of the nasal passage when pronouncing consonants.

Chapter 7

Vocal Disorders
and Voice Therapy

T O misuse our voices is the rule, not the exception. The great majority of all persons, in producing sounds, employ muscles which are not only unneeded, but which strain the vocal mechanism. Despite such common malfunctioning, many go through life with but slight vocal difficulty. Their voices may be coarse or unpleasant, or of poor quality, lacking in inflection and therefore uninterestingly monotonous. Others, because of their temperaments or their vocations, find themselves becoming hoarse, indicating chronic laryngitis or worse.

For many years, throat specialists have been concerned by the fact that functional disorders of the voice could not be treated medically. Speech therapists, too, have been aware of the problem and have done some good work in helping those with disabled voices to regain them. But usually their efforts have been concerned with aspects of the voice **after** its inception in the larynx, such as pronunciation difficulties, rather than with actual voice production. The interest of the medical profession, coupled with the efforts of speech therapists and the awareness of the problem by certain voice teachers, has led, in recent years, to the formation of a steadily enlarging group of persons whose chief concern has been with the **functioning** of the larynx and the curing of vocal disorders resulting from the abuse of its proper functions.

Many voice teachers, I am sorry to say, have tended to neglect the health of the voice in favor of demanding impressive performance of it. It is a pity when those entrusted with the care and development of the voice to its best and most glorious use show slight interest in the scientific basis for vocal hygiene. As a group, they have only recently been willing to cast aside empirical attitudes to realize that the art of singing is not art until the scientific use of the voice has been explored by them, explained to students and firmly established in their minds. They have talked far too much about the artistic results to be obtained — sometimes at great cost to the voice — and have been unduly concerned with luring the possessors of extraordinary fine voices into their studios to be pointed to as examples of their teaching. At the same time they have neglected the student of lesser natural endowment, and the possibility of his voice's being developed to its fullest and most healthy state.

During the past twenty-five years, the author has had a most unusual opportunity to treat many cases of vocal abuse in close collaboration with medical specialists. These cases have included a wide variety of disorders. The voice therapy used was based largely on the very principles already outlined in this book. The best way to convey to you what I have learned from twenty-five years of practice is to describe a few of the most significant case histories.

I have observed that voice therapy should be undertaken only by those who have studied the functions of the larynx assiduously and who have had broad personal experience in the workings of their own voices to give them the feeling of proper vocal functioning to pass on to their students. They should certainly have a working knowledge of the diseases they are treating to give them sufficient rapport with the attending physician and a common ground with the latter in proper medical terminology. Only patients referred to them by throat specialists should be treated, since it could possibly happen that a therapist might prescribe vocal exercises for a chronically hoarse patient only to find that he was suffering, not from vocal abuse, but from throat cancer. Vocal abuse may take various forms and spring from a variety of reasons. I remember reading a newspaper account of what happened in an Italian city following an exciting international soccer game; several hundred people went to throat doctors the next day because they had lost their voices! Those of you who have listened to national political conventions cannot have failed to notice how certain speakers became progressively hoarser until their voices failed entirely, simply because they had been stretching the capabilities of their voices to the vanishing point. Wendell Willkie is a classic example of a man seeking high political office whose voice refused to hold out until election day. It is easy for those who do not understand relaxation, breathing, resonance, support and their co-ordination to overtax their voices. On the other hand it is truly amazing with what ease a properly trained speaker or singer can phonate hour after hour, day after day.

Aside from physical causes for vocal failure, an important factor is what doctors call **psychological overlay.** Aside from such cases as are cited above and a good many singing students who have come to me with vocal disorders caused by pushing their voices too far, I have come to believe that a very large percentage of the patients I have treated have some psychological as well as physical reasons for their vocal inadequacies. In some cases, as you will observe in the case histories which follow, the trouble is entirely psychological.

Our voices reflect our living tensions. We have all experienced the sensation of having a "lump in the throat" when we have found ourselves under stress or have suddenly been overpowered by emotions which we could not control. At other times we may clench our teeth. It is not uncommon to awaken in the night to find ourselves grinding our jaws.

Some people have more than their share of worries; others magnify their troubles. In either case, stomach ulcers, colitis or a heart condition may result. With other people, it is the voice which is affected by tensions. There is plenty to bother us. If we are not worried about atomic fall-out or economic conditions, there is always our future security, our job, or the next payment on the television set to think about. Under these circumstances many people find their nerves wearing thin; many find their voices wearing thin.

If one has worries which are causing strain or tension which affects the voice it is obviously desirable to get rid of the **cause** of these worries. Surprisingly and gratifyingly enough, however, many times simply learning how to use the voice properly is enough to assure the patient the continued healthy use of his voice, even though he has not achieved a perfectly balanced way of life. He learns this as a **technique,** as mentioned in the golfing illustration in the chapter on breathing.

I have treated some patients who had had psychoanalytical therapy and had been greatly benefited generally thereby, but whose voice troubles had in no way responded because they still did not know how to use their voices properly. On the other hand, unbelievably simple though it sounds, there have been many cases when the patient's learning to use his voice correctly has taken his mind of his troubles sufficiently to cure him of his vocal difficulties, even though some of the psychological causes were still present.

It was in the winter of 1946, in trying to condition my own voice for a Town Hall recital, that I first applied, for curative purposes, the principles of voice production I had been applying in my teaching. Convincingly successful as this, my first experiment in therapy had been, my interest in the unhealthy throat might not have continued and grown had it not been for a combination of circumstances which almost forced me into the field.

My second step toward therapy was taken as the result of an experience with a young man who attended the music center in Massachusetts which I was directing during the summers. During the winter he was a student at a midwestern college, but had come to Duxbury in his vacation to take part in the operas and recitals which we offered as a part of our regular curriculum. I noticed that his voice, although of an exceptionally fine tenor quality, had a persistent hoarseness, and he complained that his throat became tired after he had been singing for a short time. He readily followed the directions I gave him in his singing lessons that summer, and his interest in our work together made him decide to transfer in the fall to Syracuse University, where I was teaching, and there to finish his course as a voice major.

This young man came of an extremely musical Italian background. His father was a professional musician and the son was dedicating his life to music as a singer, in spite of the very serious fault in his voice. As the summer wore on and then my work at the university began in the fall, I became more and more concerned about his hoarseness and his determination to make a career of singing. I knew that any attempts on my part to suggest a change in his vocation would be met by bitter disappointment and possibly stiff opposition. Yet as a conscientious voice teacher I simply could not go on teaching him as if his throat were normal.

In my predicament, I made an appointment for Dr. Irl Blaisdell to examine the larynx of my troubled student.

The doctor's report was made to me by letter and it was so discouraging that I did not dare to show it to the young man for fear he would jump off the nearest high building. Wrote the doctor: "Mr. A. came to see me on September —th, and examination of his larynx shows that his vocal cords are not only red and edematous, but their edges are serrated and there is considerable bowing. In my opinion this young man should change his vocation, since I do not foresee that he will ever regain a normal larynx. I believe that the cords have been greatly impaired through abuse."

This set me to thinking. The next day I telephoned the doctor, who was a good personal friend, with a proposal which I felt sure could do no harm and might produce some good results. "Irl," I said, "how would you like to go into this thing with me on an experimental basis? I have some exercises which I think could help this condition. I am willing to treat the patient and see what I can do for him in **my** way if you'll let him go to you periodically for examination and such **medical** treatment as he may need."

Dr. Blaisdell agreed readily. He, too, had been wondering about patients with functional disorders of the larynx who had been coming to him and **whom** he could not help materially as long as they continued to abuse their voices. He was far from satisfied with the standard prescription of several weeks or months of silence for these patients, since, knowing no more about how to use their voices at the end of the period than at the beginning, they only repeated their past mistakes when they recommenced to speak. The doctor showed great interest in the case and promised the experiment his full support.

Months passed. A. and I worked together several times a week, sometimes for only a few minutes, sometimes for longer periods. His voice seemed stronger, less hoarse, and as time went on, his throat muscles showed greater relaxation. He managed to maintain a high average in his other studies although he avoided ordinarily required public performances that year. Periodically he returned to Dr. Blaisdell for check-ups, but although his throat was certainly getting no worse, there was no decisive improvement in his larynx.

During this period I talked many times to the doctor, who gave me a liberal education in the structure and physiology of the phonation mechanism. He showed me motion pictures of the vocal cords working under various conditions, including abused and diseased cords. I studied the way the larynx worked and the way it **should** work and devised exercises intended to bring this about.

The following summer, A. accompanied me again to the music center on Cape Cod and continued the light, easy vocal exercises I had been giving him. As the doctor was several hundred miles away that summer, he.was not seen again until the fall. Immediately following his return to Syracuse, A. went to Dr. Blaisdell for a larynx check-up. Then my telephone bell rang and I heard the doctor's voice at the other end of the line. His exact words will never fade from my memory:

"Hello, miracle man. I wouldn't have believed it!"

"Miracle man? What do you mean?" I asked.

"A. has just been in to see me," he replied, "and his larynx is now perfectly normal. The cords are straight, white, clean — no serrations any more. A completely healthy larynx!"

So the experiment had really worked! A. went on to graduate as a voice major, after giving a fine senior recital. The next year he was given his master's degree. For over twenty years now he has been singing regularly as part of his profession in the field of music and has had no recurrence whatsoever of his voice trouble. In fact he has helped several others, by putting into practice the sort of work he and I did together, to overcome similar voice problems.

The decisive success of this case was sufficient to encourage my doctor friend to send me other functional cases which could not be treated medically. Before long we were having regular conferences and informal meetings to discuss the techniques involved. I was gaining further insight into the workings of the larynx and he was seeing demonstrations of what the new techniques could accomplish. Other members of his office group became interested and began sending me cases also. With each new case my ideas of how to treat ailing throats progressed, constantly changing for the better until they became generalized into an established pattern. My ideas of how to teach singing were affected materially and I found that what I had discovered about how to make unhealthy voices healthy applied to normal voices and helped them to grow under the most advantageous conditions.

Chapter 8

Principal Disorders of the Voice and Some Case Histories

THE vast majority of patients who have come to me for voice therapy have been suffering from vocal abuse, that is to say, misuse. Misused larynxes may manifest themselves in various ways, from slightly reddened cords to seriously damaged cords, or those which have acquired benign growths.

The most common ailment consists of cords which have become reddened and/or roughened and/or swollen (edematous) and is usually called simply **chronic laryngitis.** It is accompanied by varying degrees of hoarseness, huskiness and general tiring of the throat after sustained speaking or singing.

Bowed vocal cords are another common result of abuse or strain. The edges of the cords, instead of remaining straight, curve concavely due to incorrect muscular functioning. Thus too much air is allowed to pass between them, resulting in a chronic breathy hoarseness.

One theory to explain the muscular malfunctioning assumes that the cords are trying to perform their primitive sphincter action of closing the airway to provide additional thoracic pressure needed to meet a physical emergency. (See Appendix: Anatomy and Physiology of the Vocal Mechanism.) In other words, according to this hypothesis, not as yet fully proven, the bowing of the vocal cords is an involuntary defense mechanism.

Another relatively common complaint consists in the patient's using his **false vocal cords** or ventricular bands for phonation, along with or instead of the true cords. Sometimes, even before the true cords have come together for phonation, the false cords have met. In many cases they function so readily that it is very difficult even to see between them to catch a glimpse of the true cords. In this case the voice sounds extremely hoarse and may have a gravelly quality.

We now come to the more serious cases of vocal abuse, resulting in benign (nonmalignant) growths on the cords or on the vocal process (the point at which the cords join the arytenoid cartilages). Sometimes such growths may be hidden from view underneath the cords. The most common growth is a **vocal nodule,** commonly called "singer's node" or "preacher's node." It may occur on one or both cords, almost invariably on the anterior third, where apparently the greatest vibration occurs in phonation. The cords, instead of vibrating slightly apart, irritate each other by touching at this point until, after a while, the nodules develop, much as a corn may develop on the toe from a too-tight shoe. The growth is easily removable by voice therapy unless it is of long standing and has become especially fibrous. In such cases the doctor frequently recommends the surgical removal of only the nodule's outer surface, leaving the rest to be disposed of by therapy. In this way the cord itself remains untouched by the surgeon's knife.

Polyps or Polypoid tissue on the vocal cords are another form of benign fibrous growth which I have often treated successfully by voice therapy. They may take the form of a growth along the edge of the cord, beneath it, or there may be a single protuberance emerging from the cord on a tiny stem. There is some difference of opinion among otolaryngologists as to the exact cause of polyps, but it seems evident, from the cases I have treated and which have responded to therapy, that vocal abuse is a large factor in their formation and recurrence after surgical removal.

Contact ulcers of the larynx are due to vocal abuse and they consist generally of an ulceration on one of the arytenoid cartilages right at the vocal process where the cord is attached. There, a small protuberance, like a vocal nodule, pounds into the vocal process from the other side at the corresponding location. It is what the Doctors Jackson call "the trauma of the hammer and anvil."*This is indeed a fitting description. Such contact ulcers are limited in occurrence almost entirely to men. They may take several weeks to clear up, but voice therapy has proved to be entirely effective in getting rid of the condition.

Two other conditions treated successfully are **hysterical (spastic) dysphonia and aphonia** — partial or complete loss of the function of the voice. The causes are psychological, since the larynx is quite normal. The voice simply will not work as it should. Physical injury may enter into the case indirectly, however, as with one case I treated, in which the shock following an accident played an important part. As I have mentioned before, the very concentration on getting his voice to function properly has a psychologically therapeutic effect on the patient. One might term this psychotherapy in reverse, since turning the patient's attention to the results of his

*Jackson, C., and Jackson, C. L., **Diseases and Injuries of the Larynx,** New York, The Macmillan Company, 1942, p. 164.

trauma, whatever it may be, helps him to be relieved of its psychological, as well as its physical, effects.

Puberphonic voice, a childlike voice quality retained past puberty, is an interesting phenomenon which will be discussed in a succeeding chapter.

A good many **postoperative cases** have been sent to me — patients who, because of a laryngo-fissure (removal of one vocal cord due to carcinoma of the larynx), had undergone serious loss of voice. Therapy has proved invaluable in these cases. Special attention is given to exercises designed to cause the remaining cord to compensate by passing beyond the midline to make contact with the side of the larynx from which the other cord has been removed. A single vocal cord which has been thus developed by therapy, vibrating with or against scar tissue, produces a voice far superior to the usual very husky postoperative voice.

The treatment of **laryngeal paralysis,** in which one or both cords cannot function fully through paralysis from injury or disease, is quite similar to postoperative therapy. So long as there is the possiblity of innervation in either cord, it is possible to give the patient a better voice through strengthening the muscles which are still able to function.

Some years ago the National Association for Infantile

Paralysis referred to me a young girl suffering from bulbar paralysis due to an attack of polio. This resulted in partial bilateral paralysis of the larynx and constituted a constant danger to her health. Unable to cough up mucous or phlegm resulting from any respiratory infection, she had to have her lungs "pumped out" periodically to avoid chronic infection in respiratory areas below the larynx. My job was to teach her to cough somehow, thus overcoming the condition described. What made my task doubly difficult was the fact that she had fallen into the habit of speaking with the intake of breath on inspiration — instead of with its expulsion. Gradually, through careful work to try to strengthen any muscles which could possibly be activated in her larynx, we were able to achieve the goal of getting her rid of phlegm. At the same time she learned to speak on outgoing breath. So greatly did her voice and health improve that she was then able to resume her normal living and work.

Occupational vocal diseases occur in large numbers and many speakers and singers come to me in search of relief. Teachers, ministers, priests, rabbis, auctioneers, lecturers, entertainers, politicians, salesmen — all those who use their voices **more** than usual, or **more forcefully,** are subject to disorders of misuse, either because they do not know how to use their voices in the first place, or they do not know how to save their voices for the important occasions. You have probably known people who, when engaged in ordinary conversation, orated as if they were addressing a large audience.

Not long ago, a teaching nun came to me with chronic laryngitis. She was somewhat over forty, and although she enjoyed her work, was carrying a taxing schedule of classes for small children. Her voice had become thick and dark in color; the cords were red, rough and somewhat swollen. Formerly she had had a light high voice, she told me, but it had gradually become deep and coarse through the years as she had pushed it. She wanted very much to be able to go on with her teaching, but was afraid that soon she would have no voice at all.

We worked together for several weeks and her voice gradually rose in pitch level. As the pressures were removed and she learned how to relax the proper muscles in her throat, her voice became like that of a thirteen-year-old girl — high, light and rather weak. To the other sisters, of course, this sounded unnatural, but as time went on her voice became stronger, fuller and more mature-sounding and at her right pitch level. Finally, she came in to see me one day, and in answer to my "How are you today, sister?" she replied by **singing** in a clear firm soprano that she was just fine. Her throat no longer became tired at the end of a long day and she was able to chant during services as she had been able to do formerly. Her concentration and persistence in performing the exercises prescribed had effected this happy change, virtues I shall have occasion to stress again in these pages.

About two years ago a middle-aged produce auctioneer was sent to me in great perturbation. He was forced to use his voice hours on end every day; his livelihood depended upon its condition, and it had become almost unusable. Bowed and thickened vocal cords had made it so husky he could hardly make himself heard or understood. There was no fooling around on the part of this patient. He followed orders explicitly, meanwhile carrying on his business as usual. It took just six weeks to bring his cords back to normal and to give him back a clear, strong voice. Intermittent check-ups since that time have shown the larynx to be healthy in every way. Here was a case where "the chips were down;" the patient's vocation was at stake; there was no question in his mind as to the importance of the work we were doing together.

It would be pleasant to report that all my patients have been as conscientious as this man. Unfortunately there are some who **cannot see** the value of any treatment unless it involves "taking shots" or swallowing pills at stated intervals. They seem to have no real understanding of what a functional disorder **is,** and they sit in my presence for several sessions, expecting me to give them some miracle formula which will clear up their voice trouble overnight. They seem to expect me to do their exercises **for** them, like some of the reducing machines you see advertised. They remind me of the student who sits in the presence of a book for what he considers to be a sufficient length of time, not really concentrating upon its contents at all, but sure that somehow, possibly by osmosis, its ideas will magically infiltrate his mind and make him wise. Sometimes I have longed for a voice therapy pill for these people. And then — sometimes — through some mysterious mental process, they suddenly see the light. Just as I am about to give them up as a bad job, they fathom what I am driving at and begin really to work at their exercises, finally realizing that they are the only ones who can actually cure themselves. It seems that at first they have to be **sold** on what we are doing, perhaps by meeting another patient who has achieved a dramatic recovery, or perhaps through desperation, their doctor having told them that he can do nothing for them and that I am really their last resort.

Let me tell you of two quite similar cases, two men in executive positions in large corporations, who came to me about two years ago with the same kind of throat ailments and who well illustrate the difference between the patient who slights his exercises and the one who faithfully and systematically follows the regimen prescribed. Both men were high-powered business leaders, one considerably older than the other and presumably more "sot" in his ways. Strange to say, he was the more tractable, and it was the younger man, whom I shall call Mr. Y., and whom I shall first describe, who proved to be the "problem" patient.

Mr. Y had had an operation for the removal of polyps on his cords and had been warned by his doctor that his only chance of keeping his voice healthy was to go through a period of vocal retraining. This dynamic young man not only occupied a highly responsible position with his firm, but had the faculty and the personality to head charity drives, organize alumni functions, and generally get himself into situations where it was imperative for him to use his voice extensively. When he came to me his voice was husky in the extreme and used under constant strain. He was eager for relief but unwilling to accept any discipline which would require time, a leisurely attitude, or giving up some of his many activities. His attitude almost from the start showed that he was highly skeptical of therapy, but since his doctor had ordered it he might as well give it a try. Time after time his secretary would call me to break or postpone appointments; he had just been called into a conference, or out of town. A new appointment would be made, only to be postponed once more. He was an engaging person to meet and talk with, a happily married family man, highly respected in any endeavor he undertook, and apparently with no psychological difficulties. But it did not take me long to realize that here was a patient almost impossible to control, a man unwilling to take the time or submit to the discipline required to give his voice a chance. In business he could delegate the routine jobs to others, and he couldn't understand why his therapy couldn't be deputized. The last I heard of him was that he was about to go into the hospital for yet another operation on his larynx.

Now let me describe the case of the older man, Mr. Z. He had been under the care of several otolaryngologists. The year before he came to me, a small ulceration had developed on the middle surface of the posterior third of his right vocal cord, with inflammation surrounding it and also a slight inflammation of the opposite cord. He was put on voice rest at that time, but by March of the following year he again became **hoarse** and the ulceration reappeared in the region of the vocal process on the right arytenoid cartilage. He was fearful of throat cancer, but no malignancy was found and rest was again prescribed. For three months the trouble seemed to be disappearing, but started up again the following month. It was then that he came to me for treatment. The cord was badly inflamed.

I worked with him for two months, and then he returned to his doctor and was told that the ulcer had healed. The surface mucosa were almost intact and there was only a slight amount of granular tissue at the site of the healing ulcer. A month later he was completely cured, much to the satisfaction of his physician, who had written to me that he considered the case a difficult one indeed for voice therapy to improve. The patient went on with his business as usual. In six months he returned with a slight recurrence of his former trouble. He was somewhat husky and the cords were red. Happily he had remembered enough of our work together to need only two weeks of therapy to regain his vocal health. Since that time there has been no recurrence of the difficulty.

While Z. was undergoing treatment and had begun to regain some normal use of his voice, he came in one day and told me how he saved his voice on an unusually trying day. He would instruct his secretary: "When I give you the high-sign, tell the next person who has an appointment with me that I am having some difficulty with my voice and may not be able to talk at all." He then told of a meeting with a group of his business associates from out of town which lasted several hours and had pretty well used up his voice. After they had left, they had some afterthoughts and wanted to return for another conference. This was granted, but with the understanding that Mr. Z. would have to confine his remarks to writing. Following this "silent" discussion, my patient had enough voice left to finish out the day with needed conversation in a normal voice. This incident showed me to what lengths Z. was willing to go in complete co-operation with me and the prescribed therapy.

Therapy cases which were of purely psychological derivation puzzled me at first. My original thought was that such patients might be better off in the hands of a competent psychiatrist or psychotherapist. It did not take long, however, for me to discern that in many instances, whatever the psychological reason had been for voice trouble, the cause could have disappeared while still leaving the patient with a faulty pattern of phonation, needing guidance in the proper ways of using the voice. Once such a pattern of muscular co-ordination has been established, it is difficult for it to be erased without training and considerable conscious thought.

In 1953 a man was sent to me with a case of **hysterical dysphonia** which was interfering seriously with his responsible position in a large textile mill in northern New England. He had been troubled with this condition for over six years. Although his larynx was normal in appearance, when he began to speak, his voice would squeeze off without warning into a high squeak making him sound like an adolescent whose voice has not quite changed or an oldster who has to make a great effort to get his cords to function. He had no idea what strange sound would issue next from his throat, so that even when he didn't squeak his manner of speaking was forced and uncertain and made with great effort to push out some sort of sound which would not embarrass him.

Because many miles separated his home from my office, it was not possible for this patient to see me frequently, and accordingly it took longer for this difficulty to be corrected than would normally have been the case. After five months, however, his voice became clear, confident, of fine quality, and it served him without fail all day long in his taxing position. On one of his visits to Boston, some time later, he telephoned me and asked me if I knew who was speaking. For the life of me I could not tell. Imagine my astonishment when he told me, in firm assured tones, that he was my ex-patient of the squeaky voice.

This case differed from most vocal abuse cases I have treated, in that his voice came **down** in pitch to a resonant baritone instead of going from a croak up to a normal pleasing tone. In the elapsing years I have been gratified to find out that he has learned what to do when he feels the slightest vocal fatigue or tendency to return to his former spasmodic mode of speaking. We had given special attention to exercises for acquiring relaxation of the base of the tongue, the soft palate and the hinge muscles of the jaw, to assure the smooth and unob-structed passage of breath through nose and mouth. With this regimen, the patient has shown dramatic im-provement.

Occasionally coincidence enters into my work. Not long ago, and during the same year, two men came to me with the same rather unusual pathology — a tendency toward use of the false vocal cords, coupled with thickened and reddened true vocal cords. Both voices were thick and husky and low in pitch. One of these men was a minister who had taken on an unconscionable amount of work in his parish. Aside from the weekly sermon ("Sunday is my easiest **day**," he said to me) he had to use his voice constantly in counseling, comforting, speaking at luncheons, and talking incessantly to thoughtless parishioners who telephoned him during mealtimes. He was a cheerful person who could not help being popular and in great demand. However, this very quality served him badly in that he was being taken advantage of to the point where he was lucky to find a half-hour during the week for meditation or relaxation with his family.

The other patient was a social service director and again an extraordinarily pleasant and likeable person. He loved to talk, and his work involved speaking to groups and interviewing people all day. He found that as the day wore on, his voice would begin to leave him, and with several interviews yet to come he would push his voice until it finally became a whisper.

I do not often prescribe whispering; it is not particularly healthful and, under some conditions, may be harmful. But I asked both of these patients to whisper for a few days in the softest and most relaxed manner possible, until they had acquired some slight knowledge of what I wanted them to do with their voices. Then they began to use a soft, breathy manner of phonation, and from there we progressed to the usual treatment for such cases.

Both of these men had the same incentive, nay, necessity, to regain their vocal health, and both worked equally hard to do it. In approximately one month of concentrated effort each had regained his healthy voice and pitch level. Instead of coarse, low, croaky voices which they had used in the beginning to describe their difficulty, they turned out to possess voices of excellent tenor quality. Both have long since returned to their respective fields of endeavor and they have written several times to tell me that their voices are remaining in a fine and healthy condition, showing even further development along the right lines, as should be the case. Mutual friends also have reported that they "sound fine."

Many people feel that with advancing age their voices will naturally deteriorate as do so many of our other bodily functions. They expect to fit naturally into the "sixth age" described by Jacques in **As You Like It:**

and his big manly voice,

Turning again toward childish treble, pipes
And whistles in his sound.

As a third and final example of parallel cases described in this chapter, let me tell you about two older men who came to me a few years ago. I cite these cases to prove that old age does not necessarily mean

deterioration of the voice. The first gentleman was sent
to me for voice therapy during his three-weeks summer
vacation. He was then seventy-nine. For over forty
years, he had been Speaker of the Senate in his Midwestern state and was still an active trial lawyer. When I
first saw him, his voice was only a bare whisper from
strain. We worked together twice a day for only fifteen
days, and by that time his voice had returned to a strong,
rich bass which he was using without effort. He returned
home and I did not see him for another six months. He
told me then that when he went back to work, one of his
colleagues said that his voice sounded as it had forty
years before! Six years later, when he was eighty-five
and still practicing law, he wrote to me that "My voice is
as good as ever."

The other man was sixty-five when I first saw him and
he came to me not for voice therapy but for singing
lessons. He had sung all his life and had been a successful
tenor, confining his singing career, however, to church
work and singing for various community groups, since he
also was a busy lawyer and politician. He told me that he
had not been able to sing well for the past fifteen years
and had completely lost his upper tenor range. In fact, he
had become so discouraged with his voice that he had
given up all professional singing some time before. He

wanted to know if I could do anything with the voice of a man his age, I assured him I could help him and we worked together for a year and a half. His voice became stronger and stronger and regained its former range. At this time, I remarked at one of his lessons, "It seems to me that your voice now must be in as good shape as it was years ago." His answer was, "On the contrary. Let's face it, I was never able to use it so easily before!"

Chapter 9

Some Unusual Case Histories

IN his work with patients, the voice therapist not only deals with a variety of physical ailments, but also is faced with manifold personal problems involving the patients' background, attitudes, occupation, family relationships, economic status, and the thousand and one other factors which go to make up a human being. Inevitably he begins to sort out these elements and try to trace the vocal ailments to origins or contributing causes beyond the physical ones.

He recognizes those maladies which can be called "occupational diseases" — such as some of the cases already described. The overworked preacher and hard-pressed teacher are common types. Then there is the busy executive who spends much of his time on the telephone. He may never have learned to speak into it effortlessly, as has the switchboard operator, and thus abuses his voice constantly. Those who work under especially noisy conditions, such as one finds in certain factories where a great deal of machinery is in motion, find that the clatter and roar drown out the voice produced with normal volume and may lead to strained vocal cords. Transportation workers are a prey to this hazard. Without a great deal more know-how than most persons possess, it is impossible to shout all day long over the noise of a moving train or car, to answer the questions of passengers and call out the stops, while at the same time retaining a normal voice.

Even sex problems may be a factor. A boy in his early teens was sent to me for therapy with a diagnosis of chronic laryngitis. The cords were red and roughened. His condition was not serious, but his gravelly voice was standing in the way of his reciting in school, had been instrumental in lowering his grades, and had detracted from the general impression he made on all with whom he came in contact. His parents had sensibly realized that the problem was not solving itself, that the boy was not "growing out of it"; and they knew that this defect could seriously affect his success in any career he might choose in the future.

After interviewing the boy, I recognized that the voice he was using, aside from being so hoarse that it was inaudible at times, was being produced at a pitch level considerably lower than was natural or desirable. Gradually other factors came to light. He had an older brother whom he greatly admired and whose deep voice he wanted to imitate. He longed to be **a man.** Evidently from the moment he realized his voice was beginning to change, he had pushed its pitch down and down so he could sound more grown-up and authoritative. Though now disguised, his normal voice was fairly high and of tenor quality. I was faced with the dual problem of persuading him that there was nothing wrong or un-manly about possessing a **good** tenor voice (in fact certain tenors have been noted for their virility) and then urging him to ease up on the artificial attempt he was making to be a basso profundo. This turned out to be one of my easier "cures."

Cases of this sort have led me to wonder where this image of the deep voice as being a sign of masculinity springs from. If we look around we find that many men in high political office have voices that could in no way be called deep. Dwight Eisenhower did not have a deep voice; Abraham Lincoln is reputed to have had quite a high voice. If we keep our ears open we will be surprised to discover how many of our popular male actors do not possess deep speaking voices. Opera composers have traditionally made the hero of the piece a tenor. But, somewhere in our sociological concepts, we have come to respect depth of pitch as a sign of maturity and authority. The wish to deepen one's voice is most understandable among broadcasting announcers and speakers who find that other things being equal, the deeper voice usually transmits well with artificial amplification and is in greater demand among advertisers. This admiration for the low voice has brought many patients of both sexes to me for therapy — especially in the radio, television and entertainment fields.

While some businesswomen are content to emphasize their femininity, more frequently they tend to cultivate the forcefulness which is supposed to go with a low-register voice. In some ways this makes more sense than for a male to overwork his deep tones. This does not explain, however, why the "blues" singer with her artificially masculine voice quality should sound so attractive to so many ears. She is constantly using a quality of tone and a pitch level foreign to her feminine larynx.

Last year, one of the few successful professional singers of popular music I have treated came to me with her throat in bad condition. The cords were red and rough and she also had two vocal nodules. She was fast reaching the point where she could barely carry through her performances as a featured singer with various well-known orchestras and bands in night-club appearances.

She was singing in a manner completely unnatural to her, using what singers are apt to term a "chest voice." What they evidently mean is that the upper chest appears to play a role as a resonating cavity during the production of very low tones. It is not clearly understood as yet what actually takes place in the larynx during this sort of function. We assume that the.cords are shortened by muscle-manipulation and that possibly a larger vibrating surface is activated than the edges of the cords used during legitimate singing.

This singer was asking her vocal cords to function constantly in a manner which was not natural to them, which required muscular co-ordination foreign to her laryngeal structure and which could not be maintained without harmful results. The young lady told me that she had always had a high coloratura soprano voice until she "discovered" her popular style. It was with misgivings that I consented to try to help her to regain vocal health, for I was not at all sure that I could effect the necessary change in her larynx so long as she continued to use this unnatural voice professionally. However, I was desirous of finding out just what could be done for her by applying techniques I had been using in therapy for proper relaxation and, co-ordination. So far as she was concerned, it was a question of "either, or," since her career as a popular singer was hanging in the balance.

We worked together as often as possible—when she was able to get to Boston from out-of-town engagements; she was appearing still almost nightly in different clubs. Because she was so concerned about her voice, she worked most conscientiously on the exercises, and almost immediately she began to make sounds in our therapy sessions which indicated that her throat was in a more healthy condition. Also her extrinsic throat muscles responded extremely well to the relaxation exercises. After a while, examination by the attending physician showed that the cords were clean. The vocal nodules had disappeared. She told me that her high voice was fast returning and that she had begun to use it as part of her night-club act, meanwhile singing most of the time in her popular "chesty" voice. This intrigued her audiences and increased the versatility of her work. It showed me that, even when the method of voice production is abnormal, therapeutic exercises can assist in mitigating the ill effects.

I have not seen the young lady for six months but have had letters from her stating that she is very happy over the results achieved. I do not consider this case finished. I should like to see more of this singer to help her with the development of her natural singing voice. Also, until I have a great many more similar cases, I shall not consider that this can be chalked up as a conclusive victory. It is my hope that in the future I shall have the opportunity to work with more patients having the same difficulty and be able to help them to achieve and maintain laryngeal health.

There is apparently one major reason why women think a low female voice attractive: they have become firmly convinced that it is exotic and "sexy," especially if it is rather husky. Since the debut of Libby Holman in this role, we can point to several women in the theater who are famous for this kind of voice quality, although occasionally one reads that one of them has had to cancel performances to rest her voice. Such larynxes vary markedly in their ability to stand abuse. I have known a few women who have talked for years in an artificially low voice with no seeming ill effects. Others come to my office much worried and in great discomfort. Some are difficult to deal with since they **like** the sound of the voice they have developed and don't want to give it up. They are annoyed to have lost their voice, but are not pleased when their brighter, higher natural voice returns. A husband can be helpful in such a situation by sitting in on one of his wife's therapy sessions and hearing for himself what her vocal exercises mean; he is usually so delighted with her "new" voice, which as a steady diet is much pleasanter to listen to, that she is encouraged to try to maintain it. I remember one husband who said to his wife during one of our sessions, "Now you sound the way you did when we first started going around together."

At the opposite pole is the boy's voice which has never changed, so that at college age, or even later, the young man still retains the childlike quality of his voice. In most of these cases I have treated, the larynx looks perfectly normal. In others the patient may have acquired considerable hoarseness in a vain attempt to push his voice down to a masculine level, as described at the beginning of this chapter. There are many and complex reasons for the lack of change in a boy's voice. I am sure the pursuit of this subject would be a field day for psychologists. (A quite complete account of such reasons is given in M. Greene, **The Voice and Its Disorders,** pp. 117-123.) However, the **causes** of the lack of normal voice change may disappear but, because of the absence of the proper muscular co-ordination, the voice may remain immature. It is the work of the therapist, then, to teach the patient exercises which will develop and co-ordinate the little-used muscles and thereby draw the voice down to its normal pitch level.

The first case of this sort I treated was that of a young man of twenty-nine whose voice was frequently mistaken over the telephone for his wife's. He had three children, was employed in a responsible position, and seemed quite normal in every other way. I suppose he might have gone on for the rest of his life with his child's voice except that, not long before I saw him, he had taken up lay preaching in his spare time and his voice was just too much of a handicap. To his sorrow he had learned that he could not impart his ideas successfully to groups or congregations in a high falsetto voice.

This was my first case of the kind and it puzzled me greatly. The solution turned out to be much simpler than I had thought. After the young man had learned to relax his extrinsic throat muscles, which had been quite tense, and his voice still retained its overly high pitch, we found that by relating his breathing directly to phonation by a series of grunting sounds (produced with a properly relaxed throat but with a quick, slight inward pressure on the diaphragm each time) he was able to produce a deep, low sound, completely different in quality from his other voice. He was astonished at first, as though he were listening to someone else. He simply could not believe his ears. From this initial sound, which he was able finally to repeat each time with success by concentrating on the mechanics involved, he progressed to single words, and then to more sustained sounds.

About a week after the session just described, the young man returned for his next appointment, speaking slowly in his new-found deep voice, but wearing a rather puzzled look. Said he, "I've had quite a week. First thing that happened — when I got home from here last week and called in at the door, the children were scared to death. They were out in the kitchen where they couldn't see me and they thought a strange man had just walked into the house. All week long I've had to do all kinds of explaining every time I answered the phone and — so has my wife! And besides," he added glumly, "my throat doesn't feel so good after I've talked this way awhile."

"Don't forget," I assured him, "you're using muscles in your larynx which have never been used in this way before. I'm sure you'll find that as you use this new voice you will find this tiredness disappearing — provided you observe all the correct principles of relaxation, co-ordination and breathing. The muscles will become steadily stronger and will function finally in a perfectly normal way."

This is exactly what happened. We continued to work together for several weeks more and his voice improved every week both in quality and staying power. Since that time, several young men have come to me with this same problem and it is rewarding indeed to hear them learn to use the voice to which nature entitled them.

Unsatisfactory sexual relations can have a deleterious effect on the voice. Since the main factor in functional voice disorders appears to be undue throat tensions, anything which tends to produce or deepen such tensions can be a contributing factor in impairing the normal functions of the voice. During the past several years a few women have come to me with chronic laryngitis or the like. After we had worked together for a few sessions, and they had developed sufficient confidence in therapy and in their therapist, they spoke to me of the unhappy relations they were having with their husbands. Although they were actually in love with their husbands and wished desperately to enjoy relations with them as they formerly had, they had become frigid. One of them told me she was sure this had everything to do with her voice trouble. Why not send her, then, to a psychiatrist, you may ask? This is exactly what I suggested, with the further recommendation that the therapy be carried on in order to regain co-ordination of the larynx. In other cases, the therapy itself and concentration upon regaining the use of the voice were sufficient to enable the patient to relax and enjoy life in all its phases.

Chapter 10

Interpretation and Some Conclusions

W HY has the **interpretation** of song and speech content been left for the concluding chapter? Can your voice be at its best if what you say or sing is not given all the nuances of expression which its author intended?

Your interpretation of what you recite — with or without music — is the manner in which your brain and your heart speak for you **with your voice.** As such, the way in which you construe the meaning of the writer is a vital part of your total performance, and cannot be ignored even in such a short book as this. But I shall touch lightly upon interpretation for two reasons: first, **correct voice production is basic** — you can't build a good voice on fine interpretation, but you can develop meaningful interpretation, once you have established sound phonation techniques; second, there are scores of other teachers and writers quite as well qualified as I to write of interpretation.

To my mind, good interpretation can begin only when voice mechanics have been so thoroughly mastered that they have become second nature and need not be thought of consciously. When that point has been reached, you can choose from many fine books which treat of every aspect of the subject. And for those who want more concrete evidence of interpretation, there are thousands of superb recordings of musical works and of readings by well-known actors and poets — sometimes of their own works — which should prove to be the most revealing interpretations of all.

The first thing to study is the **intent** of the poet, dramatist or composer. This will be more readily understood when you know his background — historical, cultural, artistic and temperamental. He belongs to a certain period in time; to a certain school or clique, the members of which influenced each other, such as, for example, the Mannheim School of early symphony composers, or the French Impressionist painters, or the witty writers of the Restoration.

Perhaps, on the other hand, he was a lone genius, unheeded or misunderstood by his contemporaries, but speaking to generations to come. He may have been a giant among men, whose thoughts will seem as fresh in the coming centuries as they ever have. And there have been imitators who appealed briefly to their contemporaries but are now hopelessly dated. It is not safe to rely wholly on our intuitions. A little research to establish the setting in which the composition was hatched will well repay the trouble. Above all we must avoid the pitfall of becoming so emotionally involved in the work that, instead of presenting **it**, we present **ourselves**. No doubt you have heard young performers who became so choked with their own emotions that they have failed rightly to represent the author. The great John Mc-Cormack had the right idea when he said to keep a "cool head and a warm heart."

With popular songs it is a little different. No doubt you have heard the expression: "He can certainly **put a song over!**" And almost everyone has had the experience in a large audience of feeling that the speaker was speaking directly to **him**. The performer's own personality and magnetism may be more than half of his interpretation. When, however, the vehicle is a song of proven musical values, a fine play, or a sensitive reading, we must be careful not to get in the way of letting the work speak for itself. We do not "put over" songs by Schubert, Brahms or Debussy, nor Shakespearian soliloquies.

The true and mature interpreter remains relatively collected and detached while rendering his piece. It is we, the audience, who are carried away by the beauty of the work. The truly skillful performer has spent much time fathoming its depths and approaching it from all the angles he can imagine the composer or author having explored. Then he is ready to present it to us in such a way as to make us feel that a great light has been turned on it for our benefit. He presents it to us as it was revealed to him after prolonged emphatic study.

CONCLUSION

In closing these pages, the most helpful summary and conclusion, I think, will be to re-emphasize what I consider the most important truths I have learned and attempted to set forth.

If I could use but one word to explain all that I have learned, it would be the word **relaxation, relaxation, relaxation!** You will get nowhere until you have learned that. It sounds so easy. People say, "Just relax" — as if anyone could do it without half trying. Actually to reach complete relaxation in all of the six areas I have described, and to **stay relaxed** as the other learning steps are taken, is a tough assignment. Don't be satisfied with just partial relaxation and then proceed with the other instructions. Relaxation is both the cornerstone of the structure and the keystone of the arch. Once you have **thoroughly** mastered relaxation, the other steps are relatively easy; **until then they are impossible.** Far more than nine-tenths of all the patients who have been sent to me for therapy would never have needed treatment if they had learned thoroughly the lesson of **relaxation.**

A close second to relaxation in laying the groundwork for correct phonation is correct **breathing.** Give me a student who has thoroughly mastered relaxation and breathing and I can assure him of steady vocal improvement. I would rather wrestle with the problems arising from a student's imperfect sense of pitch, than with his inability to relax and to breathe correctly. Most flatting, due as it is to inaccurate listening, can be corrected with less frustration than a tendency to press or to breathe superficially. Support, co-ordination, resonance, color, correct phonation and lucid articulation all follow logically, once relaxation and breathing have been mastered, and then such interpretation as satisfies listener and performer alike.

There are thousands of teachers of speaking and singing and hundreds of helpful books on these matters. There would be no need for another except that now something new and vital has been added. That something is what has been learned from the first comprehensive research and experimentation in the history of phonation in which an experienced singer, speaker and teacher has worked closely with numerous throat specialists of the medical world. Voice therapy is a **new** science. We are still only just beginning to find out how much the teacher can aid the physician to correct vocal abuses and rehabilitate voices.

My experience and what I have learned have been fortuitous. I take little credit to myself for whatever pioneering I have had a hand in. No doubt there are many others who, similarly placed, would have learned as much and perhaps been more articulate in passing on their new-found knowledge. But the fact remains that I have had this good fortune, and having had it, I consider it my duty as well as my satisfaction to set down some of what I have observed.

As a teacher, the most important lesson I have learned is what can be discovered by studying the effects of a misused voice. Until I saw exactly what faulty phonation could do to a larynx and, step-by-step, worked out techniques to correct the faults, I could not rightly evaluate such needs as complete relaxation, correct breathing, and so forth. I did not know and I could not know how to avoid the pitfalls which lead to ruined voices until I had worked **backward from effect to cause,** as well as forward from cause to effect. Some of the teaching techniques which seemed good enough before I had had

this thirty-five-year "postgraduate course" in therapeutics have long since been discarded in favor of the
simpler and more vital fundamentals which I have tried
to explain in the foregoing pages.

Finally let me say, to student, teacher, choral director,
layman, and physician a few words of special importance to each.

To the Student: Make haste slowly! Do not be misled
by flashy teaching methods which bring quick and showy
results at the expense of vocal health. Beware of the
teacher whose students all sound alike, or sound too
mature when in their late teens or early twenties. If you
are young, realize that your voice is young and should
sound youthful. Let it develop as your body matures, as
your thoughts broaden and your experience deepens. Let
your own individuality come out. Don't try to sound like
other people. A typical beginner-student fault is to listen
to records and try to sound just like Jussi Bjoerling or
Renata Tebaldi or Sir Laurence Olivier. You cannot
borrow a voice; your job is to let **your** voice grow to its
full maturity under the best possible care. This applies to
drama students and to all who hope to make their ways in
the world by their voices, as well as to singers. By using a
sensible approach to your study, you may not experience
sudden or sensational development; your voice will grow
as you grow. But it will serve you well and long and **you**

will never have to worry about losing your voice.

To the Teacher: The application of science to voice teaching is still in its infancy, but the way to help your students get the most out of their voices for the longest time is to know and apply that which has been proven. Some young students with exceptional voice quality often **seem** to advance under the old empirical methods. Perhaps they have a natural knack for singing, or maybe their voices have been correctly "placed" and may seem to need little instruction save for natural development and a widening repertoire. There is great danger, however, that unless such a student or his teacher knows exactly what he is doing, he may unconsciously fall into faulty habits. You will find, moreover, that the scientific approach can produce astonishing results from even a mediocre voice.

Your student may have keen musical sense or a real flair for sensitive interpretation, but cannot count on pouring forth a glorious sound to activate his other endowments. He must therefore learn the very best use of his voice — something that cannot be mastered without a clear understanding of the physical workings of the vocal instrument. Having absorbed these fundamentals, a student with little apparent promise can become a singer or speaker of real worth. That is why I feel that it is imperative for teachers of voice to follow the discoveries and recommendations of those who have done sound research in otolaryngology in order that they may be constantly aware of the relationships between the physical mechanism and its various functions.

Although to me it seems unequivocal that speaking and singing go hand in hand, and that both should be approached with the same fundamental techniques, I recognize that this is still a controversial matter. Some time ago, in a Midwestern city, I was giving a series of talks and demonstrations on voice therapy to a mixed group of physicians, singing teachers, and teachers of speech. I hadn't even started when a speech teacher sounded off with, "I **hope,** Mr. McClosky, that you are nót going to tell us that there is a parallel between singing and speaking!" I assured the lady that that was exactly what I was going to try to prove. It is my observation that although teachers of speech have tended to be better informed than singing teachers in advances in physiological science, nevertheless the singing teacher, because he places **good sound** ahead of **clear diction,** inclines to stress correct sound production more consistently. A common fault of speech teachers, even among those well informed on the voice mechanism and its functions, is to fail to differentiate between the speaker's **resonators** and the **natural pitch** of his voice. I have had a number of speech students as patients who had been told to lower their voice pitch below the natural level in an attempt to cover up poor resonance. This can only cause strain and encourage laryngeal disorder.

It would seem that both groups — and their students — would benefit if speech teachers and singing teachers would get together oftener for an exchange of ideas and experiences. Although a teacher of singing may possibly and mistakenly permit his students to get certain vocal color effects through resonator manipulation, before the students understand what they are doing, he will recognize immediately into which **pitch** classification a voice falls. Much more often the speech teacher will try to lower a naturally high voice, rather than encouraging the student to make the best possible use of the voice which is rightfully his.

To the Choral Director: Please do not place a young singer in the wrong position in your chorus just because he or she has a rich quality of voice or reads music well. I have encountered innumerable cases of impending or acute voice-trouble, chiefly among young women, because of their having to sing as an alto instead of a soprano (their true tessitura), in a chorus. Instead of making progress during singing-lessons, we spend most of our time trying to readjust the voice to its proper teṣsitura, or, in some cases, simply **save** the voice from destruction.

Also, it would benefit your choristers if you would have them stand during a good part of their rehearsal. In my own experience as a choral-director, I have used the prescribed exercises for posture (p. 17) for my chorus-members, as well as the exercises for relaxation and proper breathing, during approximately a ten-minute period at the beginning of each rehearsal. To my mind, also, it would be **unthinkable** to ask a chorus to sing repertoire without an initial period of vocal exercises. During the times your chorus-members are **sitting** during the rehearsal, ask them to sit on the edge of their chair, with their spine straight, thereby approximating a standing posture insofar as it is possible.

To the Layman: Though you may not be a teacher, choral director or a student, if you are interested enough in your voice at its best to have read thus far, you must recognize how much a pleasing and easily produced voice can add to the life of everyone — yourself and all who hear you. You can hardly have failed to benefit from what you have read already. The concepts of relaxation and breathing alone set forth herein should consciously and observedly improve your speaking or singing voice. More important still, if you follow the simple instructions given, you need not fear that your voice will give out when perhaps you need it most.

To the Physician: The techniques I have described have now been well tested and proven valuable as therapeutic aids. They cannot be entirely self-taught nor left completely to the patient for study. It is still the exceptional community in which there is not available a singing or speech teacher who is presently qualified to work with otolaryngologists as a few of us have done. But perhaps this book may be of some help to you in finding a teacher of voice in your locality who, with additional training in therapy techniques, could assist you to rehabilitate the voices of some of your patients who are suffering from vocal disorders.

To All My Readers: This book in no way purports to offer dazzling new discoveries about the voice and its workings. It is rather a synthesis of findings and ideas gleaned over a long period of years from many sources and much experience. No amount of theory will take the place of **honesty** in the teacher or **common sense** in the student. Use your voice; do not abuse it. Steer clear of glamorous approaches, double-talk and charlatanry. Your voice is a miracle in itself; do not expect miracles of it. I can only hope that in these few pages I have helped to clarify your ideas about the voice and pointed the way to its best use.

The human voice is still evolving from a "valve" to the most perfect and versatile musical instrument. Considering that it began with grunts, growls, barks, screeches and other animal cries, we have come a long way. Now we know that science can help us to go much farther, and we know some of the ways in which science can help us to speak and sing better. In this evolution, the correction of faults and the curing of voice malaise have taught us much about how to speak and sing in the first place. Working from **result to cause** is the one out-standingly **new** approach which I hope will make this book a valuable contribution to both art and science.

Appendix

Anatomy and Physiology of the Vocal Mechanism

IT may seem strange to some of my readers that I have not placed this section at the beginning of the book instead of almost at the end. It is not because the section was an afterthought but because I did not think it absolutely necessary to the preliminary understanding of the rest of the book. I have tried to make each chapter self-explanatory in its particular field, with the emphasis on how the larynx **functions** rather than on how it is **made.** A few basic facts about the laryngeal cartilages, muscles and nerves may prove helpful, however, to your understanding of their function and throw light on the phenomenon called "voice" which we are so apt to take for granted.

As we study the larynx (or, as it is sometimes **called** colloquially, the "voice box") it is obvious almost from the beginning that, unless we have had a good deal of medical training, it will be difficult to understand this complicated and detailed mechanism. It is not my wish to mire the reader in a mass of technical names and terminology which are entirely strange to him, but if we are to gain even a fair knowledge of the voice beyond vague, empirical generalities, we should know something about the area where it originates. In this chapter, therefore, I shall attempt to make as simple and yet complete an explanation as possible of the larynx and the way it operates. For those who wish to pursue the study further, I suggest excellent chapters*in some of the works listed in the bibliography, and the very complete pamphlet by Dr. Pressman and Dr. Kelemen, with its own large bibliography.

Perhaps the best way to understand the larynx is to realize right from the beginning that we are dealing with a mechanism which was not intended to produce sounds at all, but rather to keep foreign matter out of the lungs, and when needed, to keep air trapped in them when extra

* M. Greene, **The Voice and its Disorders,** Chapter 3.

Gray and Wise, **The Bases of Speech,** pp. 168-187 and 336-338.

Negus, **The Comparative Anatomy and Physiology of the Larynx,** Chapter 2.

†Pressman, J.J., and Kelemen, G., **Physiology of the Larynx.**

thoracic pressure is needed for lifting, hugging, climbing, and so forth, or when abdominal pressure is needed for such matters as childbirth or elimination. It began as a rather simple sphincter mechanism (ring of muscle with the power of contraction such as those surrounding the anus). In the few thousand years during which it has been evolving toward its added present function in speech and song, the larynx in man has undergone a great deal of change, synonymous with his emerging from the water, living on the ground, taking to the trees and coming back again to being a ground-living animal. As man climbed away from the ground and into the trees to get away from his enemies or seek out a new food supply, he acquired an upright posture, better eyesight and less sense of smell than he had needed when sniffing along the ground. As he came to depend more on his sight, his long soft palate and movable epiglottis (which had been used to come together and direct air solely through his nose, so that even while eating or with his mouth open, he had his full powers of scent) degenerated so as to become almost useless as an aid to smelling. Meanwhile, his larynx gradually changed to adapt to his changing needs. By the time he had again descended from the trees, his larynx had altered from its original purposes a good deal but had become adapted more satisfactorily to making sounds. As he developed intellectually and physically, he acquired the ability to make more complicated and varied sounds and then to produce speech and song.

At our present stage of evolution, the larynx consists of a skeleton of interdependent cartilages in the neck attached above (superiorly) to the **hyoid bone.** (This is a slender, curved bone lying just under the chin at the base of the tongue in a position somewhat like that of a horseshoe with its center at the front. See Figure 4, p. 120, Figure 5, p. 121, Figure 7, p. 123.). The hyoid bone in turn is attached by muscles and ligaments to the base of the tongue, the lower jaw and to points in the neck just below the ears. The larynx is attached by muscles and ligaments below (inferiorly) to the breastbone, or sternum. The muscles which serve to anchor the larynx into the neck are called, as a group, the **extrinsic** muscles of the larynx and I shall not go into their names or functions here except to say that most of them are apt to come into play in the acts of swallowing or phonating. It is their action in phonation which we wish to minimize as much as possible. (For a clearer idea of their position and structure, see Figure 6, p. 122.)

The cartilages of the larynx are nine in number, but again we need not concern ourselves in this book with more than five. Starting at the bottom, there is the

cricoid cartilage. As its Greek name implies, it resembles a finger ring and is almost always referred to as being in the particular shape of a signet ring with the signet turned around toward the back (see Figures 4 and 5, pp. 120, 121). Above it, and connected to it by membranes, ligaments and muscles, lies the **thyroid** cartilage, the largest of the laryngeal cartilages. The front of it is shaped rather like two shields (as its name again indicates) which are joined together in the middle to form the "Adam's apple" at its upper end. It is open at the back, and from each corner, so to speak, projects a cornu, or horn, two reaching upwards and two extending downwards. (See Figures 4, 5, and 7; pp. 120, 121, 123.) The upper ones connect with the hyoid bone and the lower ones connect with the cricoid cartilage. Jointed also to the upper part of the front wall of the thyroid cartilage is the **epiglottis,** also a cartilage. (See Figure 7.) We come at last to the final two cartilages which we shall discuss, and those which directly control the vocal cords. These are paired and are called the **arytenoids.** They lie on the top of the "signet" portion of the cricoid cartilage and inside the back of the thyroid cartilage. (See Figure 7.) Their name means that they are ladle-shaped, but actually they are better described as being in the shape of two small pyramids. The arytenoid cartilages are capable of pivoting in and out and approximating or separating from each other, and it is through their movement that the vocal cords change position, since the cords are attached to them (the point of attachment being called the **vocal process**). (See Figure 8, p. 124.) The space between the cords is known as the **glottis**.

The muscles which are connected with and ╱or cause the vocal cords to function are referred to as the **intrinsic** muscles of the larynx. These muscles serve in different capacities to bring the cords together (adduction) or cause them to separate for breathing space (abduction) or they cause the cords to become taut or lax to produce pitch changes. With their action and interaction, there is an almost infinite variety of possibilities for changing the shape, length and thickness of the cords. There still appears to be some confusion as to exactly where some of their functions lie and I do not wish to confuse the reader by too much concentration on this physiology, which is still open to question. Figure 10, p. 126, should be of some help in showing their position, however. Keep in mind the fact that muscles are named by their points of attachment and that the muscles of which we are speaking at present all come in pairs except one, which is the **transversus** or **inter-arytenoid**.

The **crico-thyroid** muscles run between the cricoid and

thyroid cartilages anteriorly, and when they contract, they change the relationship of one cartilage to the other (that is, the cartilages are pulled closer together in front) and, in consequence, the vocal cords which are attached in front to the inside of the thyroid cartilages are lengthened and made tighter or more taut.

The other four major muscles have as at least one of their points of attachment the **arytenoid cartilages.** They are called:

The **thyro-arytenoids**
The **posterior crico-arytenoids**
The **lateral crico-arytenoids**
The **inter-arytenoid**

The **thyro-arytenoid** muscles are attached in front to the inside of the thyroid cartilage and at the rear to the arytenoid cartilages. They lie horizontally across the larynx and it is their thin edges themselves which we call the **vocal cords.** These muscles also act in contraction to shorten the cords. Lying above each vocal cord is a fold composed of glandular, muscular and other tissue which is known as the **ventricular band** or **false vocal cord.** They are separated from the true cords by a horizontal air sac known as a **ventricle.** They aid the valvular processes of the larynx by helping to trap air in the lungs when necessary. They may be seen very clearly in

Figure 11, p. 127.

The **posterior** and **lateral crico-arytenoid** muscles, when working together in the proper co-ordination, assist each other in bringing the cords together. (Figure 9, p. 125) In many cases of vocal abuse, however, they may act independently so that the posterior muscles attempt to force the cords apart producing bowing and the lateral muscles bring the vocal processes together, producing an open posterior chink. In either case, careful vocal exercises are required to make the cords straight again.

The **inter-arytenoid** acts to bring the arytenoid cartilages themselves closer together and therefore, of course, to approximate or adduct the cords.

All these muscles are innervated for **motion** by the **recurrent laryngeal nerve,** except the crico-thyroid, whose innervation comes from the **superior laryngeal nerve** which also supplies **sensory** innervation to the interior of the larynx. (See Figure 12, p. 128.)

At first reading, this chapter may seem confusing to anyone unused to medical terminology or discussions of physiology and anatomical structure. If the reader will bear with me, however, and refer faithfully to the figures mentioned, I am sure that on a rereading, he will find the whole picture of the larynx, its anatomy and functions becoming clearer in his mind and aiding him in the study of his voice and its development.

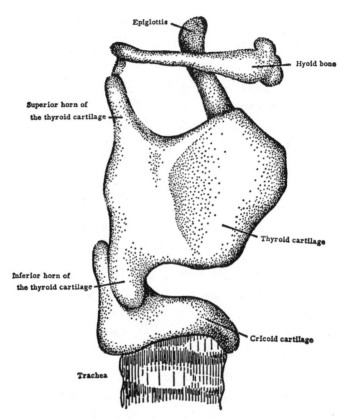

Epiglottis

Hyoid bone

Superior horn of
the thyroid cartilage

Thyroid cartilage

Inferior horn of
the thyroid cartilage

Cricoid cartilage

Trachea

FIG. 4.   The Hyoid Bone and Cartilages of the Larynx

(Lateral View)

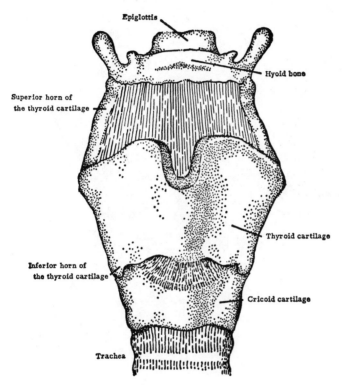

Epiglottis

Hyoid bone

Superior horn of the thyroid cartilage

Thyroid cartilage

Inferior horn of the thyroid cartilage

Cricoid cartilage

Trachea

FIG. 5. Anterior View of the Cartilages of the Larynx

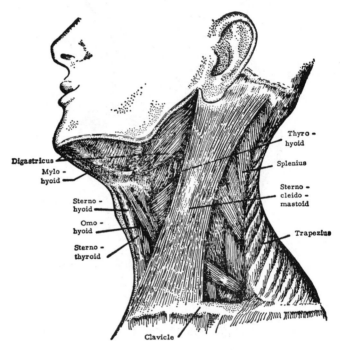

FIG. 6. Extrinsic Muscles of the Larynx

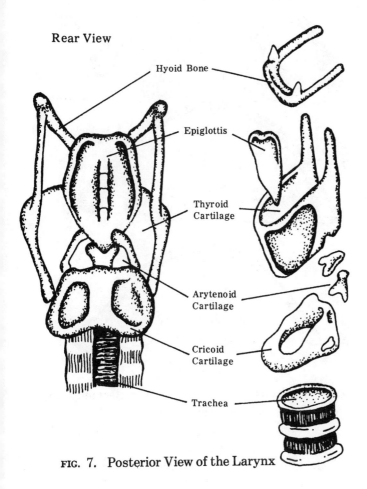

Rear View

Hyoid Bone

Epiglottis

Thyroid
Cartilage

Arytenoid
Cartilage

Cricoid
Cartilage

Trachea

FIG. 7. Posterior View of the Larynx

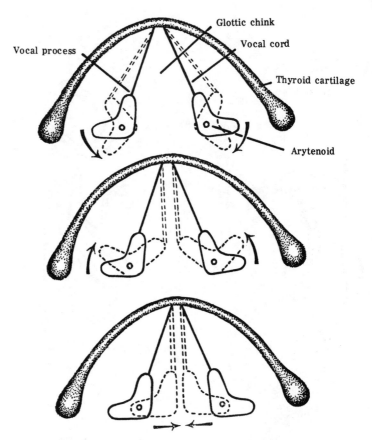

FIG. 8. Horizontal View of the Larynx, Showing Action
of the Arytenoids:

A. *Vocal cords moving from gentle to full abduction*

B. *Vocal cords moving from gentle abduction to adduction*

C. *Vocal cords moving from gentle abduction to position for phonation*

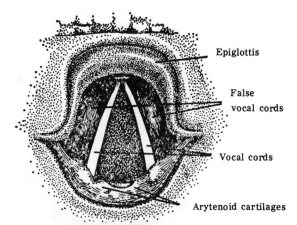

Epiglottis

False
vocal cords

Vocal cords

Arytenoid cartilages

(a) Vocal cords in quiet breathing

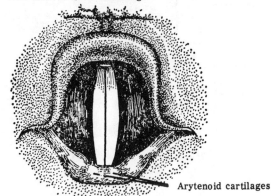

Arytenoid cartilages

(b) Vocal cords in phonation

FIG. 9.   Vocal Cords as They Appear in the Laryngeal Mirror

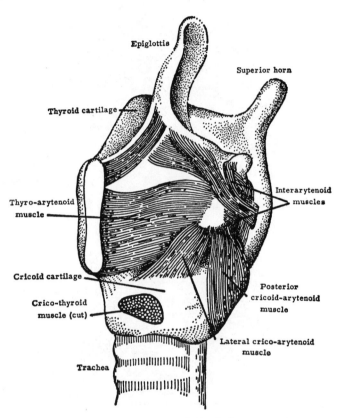

Epiglottis

Superior horn

Thyroid cartilage

Interarytenoid muscles

Thyro-arytenoid muscle

Cricoid cartilage

Crico-thyroid muscle (cut)

Posterior cricoid-arytenoid muscle

Lateral crico-arytenoid muscle

Trachea

FIG. 10. Intrinsic Muscles of the Larynx

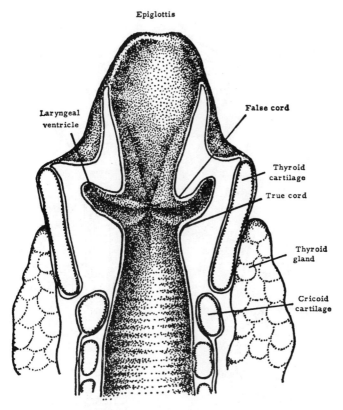

Epiglottis

Laryngeal
ventricle

False cord

Thyroid
cartilage

True cord

Thyroid
gland

Cricoid
cartilage

FIG. 11.   Frontal View of the Larynx, Showing Position of the
False Vocal Cords

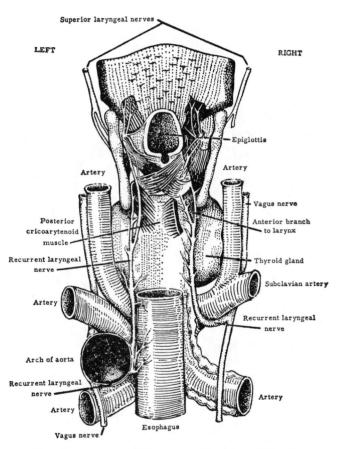

Superior laryngeal nerves

LEFT

RIGHT

Epiglottis

Artery

Artery

Vagus nerve

Posterior
cricoarytenoid
muscle

Anterior branch
to larynx

Recurrent laryngeal
nerve

Thyroid gland

Subclavian artery

Artery

Recurrent laryngeal
nerve

Arch of aorta

Recurrent laryngeal
nerve

Artery

Artery

Vagus nerve

Esophagus

FIG. 12.   Innervation of Intrinsic Muscles of the Larynx

Bibliography

Breuer, Josef, and Freud, Sigmund, **Studies on Hysteria** (tr. by James Strachey in collab. with Anna Freud), New York: Basic Books, Inc. 1957.

Bachner, Louis, **Dynamic Singing**, New York, A.A. Wyn, Inc., 1944.

Brown, William Earl, **Vocal Wisdom**, Maxims of Giovanni Battista Lamperti, Pub. by author, 1931.

Craig, William C., and Sokolowsky, Ralph R., **The Preacher's Voice,** Columbus: The Wartburg Press, 1946.

Fields, Victor A., and Bender, James F., **Voice and Diction,** New York: The Macmillan Company, 1949.

Gray, Wilkeson, and Wise, Claude Merton, **The Bases of Speech** (rev. ed.), New York: Harper and Brothers, 1946.

Greene, Harry P., **Interpretation in Song,** New York: The Macmillan Company, 1921.

Greene, Margaret, **The Voice and Its Disorders,** New York: The Macmillan Company, 1957.

Haslam, W. E., **Style in Singing,** New York: G. Schirmer, 1911.

Henderson, W. J., **The Art of the Singer,** New York: Chas. Scribner's Sons, 1906.

Jackson, Chevalier, and Jackson, Chevalier L., **Diseases and Injuries of the Larynx,** New York: The Macmillan Company, 1942.

Lederer, Francis L., **Diseases of the Ear, Nose and Throat** (6th ed.), Philadelphia: F. A. Davis Co., 1952.

Monroe, Alan H., **Principles of Speech** (brief ed.), Chicago: Scott, Foresman and Company, 1945.

Negus, V. E., **The Comparative Anatomy and Physiology of the Larynx,** London: William Heinemann Medical Books, Ltd., 1949.

Pressman, Joel L., and Kelemen, George, "Physiology of the Larynx," American Academy of Ophthalmology and Otolaryngology, reprinted from **Physiological Review,** Vol. 35, No. 3, July, 1955, pp. 506-554.

Vennard, William, **Singing, the Mechanism and the Technique** (revised edition), New York: Carl Fischer, Inc., 1967.

Watson, Floyd R., **Sound,** New York: John Wiley and Sons, Inc., 1935.

Wilcke, Eva, **German Diction in Singing** (tr. by Arthur Edward Smith, M.D.), New York: E. P. Dutton and Co., Inc., 1930.

Zerffi, William A. C., "The Laryngologist's Place in Advising Vocalists," **Musical America,** Jan. 1, 1952, p. 25.

Zerffi, William A. C., "Voice Reeducation," **Archives of Otolaryngology,** Nov., 1948, Vol. 48, No. 5, pp. 521-526.

Zerffi, William A. C., "Laryngology and Voice Production," **Annals of Otology, Rhinology & Laryngology,** 1952, Vol. 61, No. 3, pp. 642-647.

Acknowledgments

I T seems most appropriate first to express my gratitude to those members of my immediate family who set me on the way to a career in singing and teaching. They were all professional singers and teachers themselves whose example made it natural for me to follow them — my mother, and incidentally my first teacher, May Blair McClosky; my father, D. Byron McClosky; my aunt, Rose Blair Delano; my grandmother, Susan Blair; and my great-uncle, Walter Blair.

During my early years in Boston, Miss Heloise E. Hersey offered me invaluable encouragement, both moral and material, as well as the benefit of her superior cultural background. I should like also gratefully to acknowledge the good influence of my teachers, Charles Bennett, Emily Ellis and Rodolfo Fornari in Boston, and Fernando Tanara in Milan, Italy, as well as the wise counsel and support of Dr. Ernst Victor Wolff, who acted as coach and accompanist for me in Berlin and New York. I am indebted also to many colleagues for their co-operation and encouragement — Oren Brown, Alexander Kipnis, Grace Leslie, Radiana Pazmor, Aksel Schiøtz and Priscilla Sprague.

So far as my work in voice therapy is concerned, it would be impossible for me to express adequately my indebtedness to the late Dr. Irl H. Blaisdell of Syracuse, New York. His interest in therapy, as regards both research and application, opened up for me a new world of ideas about the voice. I should like also gratefully to acknowledge the encouragement given me by two other Syracuse otolaryngologists, Dr. Gordon D. Hoople and Dr. David W. Brewer, as well as by Dr. Theo Walsh of St. Louis.

Dr. Leroy A. Schall made further study and work in voice therapy possible for me at the Massachusetts Eye and Ear Infirmary in Boston. Dr. George F. Reed was a guiding light as research advisor and head of the voice therapy clinic at the Infirmary. Also, because of their continued interest in my work, which they have expressed by repeatedly sending me patients, I should like to express my warm thanks to Drs. C. H. Ernlund, John R. Frazee, Robert L. Goodale, Arthur J. Gorney, Edgar M. Holmes, Vincent J. Kelley, G. D. King, Robert E. Klotz, Donald K. Lewis, M. H. Lurie, P. E. Meltzer, Daniel Miller, William W. Montgomery, John R. Richardson, Frank R. Schlossberg, H. J. Sternstein, Morris Swartz, Sidney R. Wilker, Robert H. Lofgren, Peter Oliver, J. Wilbur Gould and Werner Chasin.

I am grateful to Mrs. Ruth G. Mitchell for her contribution to the assembling of the final manuscript, and to Harry Silberman for his kindness in preparing the vocal exercises.

Without the firm guidance and professional advice of Frank W. Nye, this book could not have appeared.

Last, I am grateful to my very good friend and publisher, Paul W. Bittinger, for his patience, care and assistance in the preparation of these four paper-back editions.

Only a few names have been mentioned of the hundreds of people who have offered me ideas, advice and friendly support. My thanks to them all.